LIVING IN THE KEY OF JOY

Stories and inspiration to make your heart dance and your spirit sparkle

PRESENTED BY
GAIL CLANTON

Cover design by Janet Harward, JanetDesign
janetharward.myportfolio.com

ISBN 978-0-578-90793-2

LIVING IN THE KEY OF

JOY

Stories and inspiration to make your heart dance and your spirit sparkle

Presented by Gail Clanton

DEDICATION

I dedicate this book to my mother and the mothers of each woman who has a story included in this collection.

We honor them with our stories of joy.

TABLE OF CONTENTS

FOREWORD

In the midst of a global pandemic that was taking countless lives... in the midst of political unrest that was challenging the very fabric of our nation... and in the midst of racial injustices that were personal and painful... 21 women stepped out to tell stories of healing, faith, happiness, and joy.

It is our hope that you will be inspired by our stories and that you will be encouraged to do what you can to keep your own sense of joy intact; no matter what.

My Joyous Journey

"A Joyful Heart is Good Medicine"
Proverbs 17:22

By Diane Ables

My Joyous Journey

"A Joyful Heart is Good Medicine"
Proverbs 17:22

By Diane Ables

My Joyous Journey reflects upon how I have changed the "whys" of my life into "why nots"! It is my prayer that readers will be encouraged, enlightened, entertained, and empowered by reading my story.

I acknowledge my wonderful Mom, the late **Marian Moseley Price**, who gave me so much unconditional love. Also, I appreciate the support from Gail Clanton, the visionary for this book, and all the other co-authors.

My story will focus on the following four chapters of my life:

1. My Formative Years
2. My Conformative Years
3. My Informative Years
4. My Transformative Years

My Formative Years. I was five and my sister was seven years old when our family structure changed as a result of the divorce of our Mom and Dad. My Mom, Grandma, my sister and I moved to another city. My father remained in the family home. He remarried and our Stepmom made sure we spent quality time with my Dad. I knew this chapter of my life would not be a "crystal stair", yet I have always walked to the beat of a different drummer and knew that I'd be fine.

Our Mom set the tone in our household with strict rules about social graces, manners, and keeping our rooms clean. My Mom became the primary breadwinner. I truly admired her strength, tenacity and determination to move forward in life with such grace. In my younger years, I recall that my sister bathed me with a scrub brush and Ajax cleanser. My Mom asked her why she did this to me, my sister replied, "You told me to get her clean."

My Grandma was our daytime caregiver. Grandma was such a delightful person in so many special ways. She loved to cook. I remember her delicious homemade cookies that spread together and looked like a sheet cake. Unfortunately, there came a time when our Grandma needed specialized attention in a skilled care facility. This happened when my sister and I were teenagers, and my older sister took on the role of being my caregiver.

My Conformative Years. During this stage in my life, I became somewhat rebellious about following so many rules. I did not follow the traditional path and at 18 I was married. I did finish high school with my class, yet I felt a tremendous void in my life. So, with a lot of determination, I successfully passed the Civil Service exam typing requirement of 45 words per minute on a manual typewriter. "Why work so hard to achieve this goal?" you may ask. Why not?

I entered the world of work beginning as a Clerk Typist and successfully moved up the career ladder to a higher professional series. During this time, I furthered my education by earning my Bachelor of Science and Master of Arts degrees in 13 years, all while working full time. These changes in my life caused a tremendous breakdown in communication with my husband. We divorced after 17 years of marriage and two wonderful children. We both agreed to make our daughter and son our number one priorities. Proudly, our daughter and son have successfully earned degrees and are gainfully employed.

My Informative Years. I have maintained so many relationships that have made a positive impact in my life!

I have an insatiable need to learn and "think out of the box" and I do so with the help of these numerous friends who are so diverse in age and marital status. One dear friend speaks with such a commanding manner and she often says to me "Diane, I am going to take those sticks away from you". She was speaking to the fact that I often discredit my capabilities.

It was during this time that I again challenged myself to turn a "why" into a "why not" and I took an early retirement from the government and pursued other career options.

My Transformative Years. At the age of 50, having just retired, I had so many adventures planned. For example, for my 50th birthday, a friend and I planned my birthday celebration. Now, the best laid plans sometimes do not work out. Four hours before the party, I did not realize that my patio was a sheet of ice. So, with a handful of party decorations, I fell on the ice. I was in total disbelief to realize that my left ankle was severely injured. Subsequently, I was in the hospital having emergency surgery on my left ankle while my 50th birthday party went on. My son wrote on my enlarged birthday card "Well Mom as they say in Hollywood, the show must go on". When I saw my birthday party video, I knew without a doubt that everyone enjoyed this joyous celebration without me. I learned "not to fly faster than my guardian angel has wings."

During this chapter in my life, I experienced many different careers, from being a partner in a counseling center to substitute teaching. When these options were presented to me, I didn't ask myself "why?" Instead, I asked "why not?"

Each of my career positions enabled me to become more compassionate, emphatic, and to enhance my sense of humor. One of my most joyous work experiences was as a substitute teacher with kindergarteners. I learned that **"the time out"** was when you had to **"sit in a chair"**. I also learned a **torn** piece of paper was **broken**!

I am so filled with joy that my son has married a loving and sweet-spirited lady and they have given me 4 handsome grandsons. The oldest grandson has taught me so much about moving into the 21st century. He questioned me about why I had only four channels on my TV. Hence, **I got cable**!

One day, this very witty, energetic grandson was getting on my last nerve. As we entered a church where a yoga class with going on, this grandson said "Grandma, you need to get in a yoga class to calm your nerves." I wanted to ask him why, but instead I thought to myself, "why not?" I have been in yoga class for over 20 years.

This wonderful grandson has also introduced me to NETFLIX and given me a tablet. The other three grandsons have also challenged Grandma with technology.

When they come to visit, I always prepare a good homemade meal. Grandma's usual bedtime is 10pm. The grandsons' bedtime is about midnight or thereafter. Their favorite thing to do with Grandma, while she is sleeping, is putting a blue tooth on her bed playing music or singing "**Granny Dandy**". I am so looking forward to the day when my grandsons have children. I will definitely share my experiences with my great grandchildren about **their fathers**!

Now, my loving daughter has taken on the role of being my mom. I chuckle at how she mimics some of my ways and questions situations like I would. I have also connected with so many progressive women in their 50's who are authors and entrepreneurs. I enjoy learning so much from them about embracing change. I also have two seasoned married couples in my life who demonstrate what real love Is about!

During my joyous journey I have experienced so many emotions; joy, pain, doubt, worry, fear, and anxiety. But, without a doubt, **JOY**, is my mantra. Why JOY? Why not?

God's richest blessings to all!

Joy Disguised As An Ugly Dress

By Claudette Abney

Joy Disguised As An Ugly Dress

By Claudette Abney

She had that look on her face. You know it. That look parents display when they are so proud of a goal they have accomplished for you; something that you did not even know you wanted. I had a look on my face too. It was the look children get when they sense their parents are about to reveal something and that they know nothing about. Is it big or small, wonderful, or not so great at all? So, I braced myself.

Then, it happened. My mother, with a big smile on her face and smizing eyes aimed at drawing me in, opened a bag and pulled out "The Dress," the very thing I dreaded. But there it was, in all its, no, not splendor -- ugliness.

"Dear Lort!" Yes, Lord with a "t" instead of a "d." Lort! It was brown, chocolate brown. This is significant because I am brown, chocolate brown. Do you see what I saw? I was about to be a walking, moving muted shade of brown at eight years old. I was being dulled down in the worst way possible – through fashion. Fashion is supposed to speak. At eight years old my fashion was in jeopardy of being silenced before it had begun to express itself. To add insult to injury, someone had an epiphany, some divine revelation from where I do not know, that it would be a good idea to put daisies all over this brown dress. GIANT daisies. No designer there.

Now, in my Rod Sterling Twilight Zone* voice, “Picture this:” An eight-year-old girl about four feet five inches tall weighing maybe seventy pounds, with legs that look like tiny tree branches peeking out from beneath this brown dress with the giant daisies and little green leaves sporadically placed on “The Dress” without rhyme or reason. Did I mention that “The Dress” was two sizes too big? I’m thinking, “What the heck was *she* thinking?”

But here’s the wonderful thing... At eight years old, I had enough wisdom not to make a fuss, to just wear the ugly dress. That wisdom came from that smile on my mother’s face and that look of satisfaction in her eyes. I was not going to hurt my momma’s feelings. So, Sunday after Sunday, with hardly a word passing between us, we went to church, she wearing her favorite hat and me wearing “The Dress,” that ugly dress. Thank God I liked my shoes and purse. Ah, the comfort of accessories.

Fast forward to age 26. I’m at work and I get a call from my mother. Immediately, I hear that look on her face, as she is summoning me to come to her house after work. She wants to show me something. “Dear Lort.” With a “t” again! I agreed to come over. However, I am praying silently in my heart and my head, “Father, please don’t let there be another ugly dress. I cannot go through that again. This time, I am going to just hurt her feelings and she’s going to have to deal with it.” This soundless conversation with myself goes on for the next three and one-half hours, as I stress over what I am going to find at mom’s house. “Say it ain’t so, Lord. Say it ain’t so!”

I arrive and she is waiting for me. Yep. There’s that look I heard over the phone three and one-half hours ago and the look I saw on her face eighteen years ago. I go into the house, following up the stairs behind her. I am counting these stairs slowly. I have never counted these stairs before. When Mom got to the top of the stairs, she started gliding toward her bedroom like she was a movie star. I, on the other hand, am standing still on the landing questioning in my mind, “What the devil?” (My mom’s favorite expression when she was angry or didn’t know what was going on.)

Before she enters the room, she turns and motions, “Come on, come on,” while nodding her head up and down. I’m thinking, “No Mom. Just no.” I called on the ancestors for courage, paused, took a deep breath, and entered that room, I was full of dread.

“You’d better get the heck outta here!” I delightedly exclaimed before I realized I was even speaking. Mom was sitting on her bed beside the most beautiful pure silk red bathrobe. She was smiling joyfully from ear to ear as she said, “This is for you Little Bit.” In that moment, there were no words spoken by either one of us. None were needed. None could have captured that moment. The love in that room was so thick it was palpable.

In that very moment, I realized Mom had known the whole time that I hated that ugly, two sizes too big brown daisy dress and had spent the past eighteen years waiting for an opportunity to make up for it. And I, well, I realized that "The Dress," that ugly dress, was all she could afford at the time. It was what she had then to express her love to me, her beloved daughter. Finally, able to speak, I asked her what was going on and she said, "I got upgraded. You got upgraded too. We go up together." OH, HOW GREAT MY JOY! Go ahead. You can cry. I did.

Decades later, while engaging in retail therapy, I round a corner in a clothing store and what do I see. No. It can't be. Yes, it can and it was -- "The Dress," in all its SPLENDID "ugliness". Stop it! LOL! Instantly, I knew it was my mother. I grabbed that ugliness in a hurry, rushed to the dressing room, put it on and cried and laughed at the same time, while styling in the mirror.

You do know I bought that ugly dress, right? It's hanging in my closet, never to be removed. Each time I look at it, I feel a wink in my soul from the woman known simply as Mom.

The moral of this story: Choose love. Wear the ugly dress. Who knows what hidden joy it may hold?

“Many women do noble things; but, you surpass them all” (Proverbs 31:29 NIV). Thanks Mom. You brought me love -- and JOY -- disguised as an ugly dress.

---

*Twilight Zone was a 1959 series created and hosted by Rod Sterling.

On The Third Day

Yvonne Allsopp

On The Third Day

By Yvonne Allsopp

Why do some of us make poor food choices? Since I know that fried chicken, cheesecake, and unsalted potato chips are not healthy, why did I consume them?? I don't know why! Denial? Afterall, I included *unsalted* chips! But I do know that my recent 3rd Day Experience, has shaken me to the core! I had a STROKE!

In May 2019, my daughter, Beryl, and I were preparing for the daunting task of moving from our birth state of New York to North Carolina. Beryl, her friend, and I had gone out to lunch. After eating, I felt dizzy and then my head hit the table! I was only out for a few minutes, but because I could walk and talk, I refused to allow anyone to call an ambulance. After much discussion, I agreed to go to an Emergency Room. I was anxious, but all that was on my mind was the move. I had not moved in nearly 20 years, so you can only imagine the situation that confronted us.

After hours of poking and questions in the ER, I was diagnosed with a TIA. A TIA is a transient ischemic attack, or a mini stroke. This means that there was a brief interruption of blood to my brain. I felt like I was in a fog, no pain but a bit dizzy. I was worried about what was happening to me. Would I still be able to move? When the ER doctor told me that I could go home, but to be sure to follow up with my Primary Care Physician the next day, I was so relieved.

Once home, I only wanted to sleep and then resume packing. I did, however, go to my doctor the next day and I was given new cholesterol medications. I hate medications and now I was adding another one to my growing list. I was already taking high blood pressure meds, now I was adding cholesterol pills. How did this happen? Well, I had too much to do to overly concern myself with this TIA. I bargained with myself that if I ate more green veggies with the mac and cheese, I would be fine!

Fast forward to, December 16, 2020, Wednesday am.

I awakened, no pain; felt weird. Dizzy, my legs felt like lead, my left ankle swollen. My feet and arms were tingling. My entire body was hot, I took my temperature. It was 97degrees, no fever, but I knew something was wrong because when I tried to grasp something in my hand, I could not feel anything. My hand was numb.

I carefully got my wallet. I knew I needed to talk with a medical professional. I called the Nurse Line number printed on the back of my insurance card. I spoke with a nurse who insisted that I needed immediate care. "Oh no", I thought to myself, "I will have to awaken Beryl, she will be so worried! Lord, why?" We have a cat, he will be afraid. I couldn't find my socks. It's raining outside. I didn't want to go to an ER, there was the Covid virus and many people who went to emergency rooms never left the hospital. These thoughts flooded my mind!

Within minutes, there were seven strangers in our apartment! The cat hid, someone was talking to Beryl, and two of the strangers were attending to me. They asked a copious number of questions. All I could think of was, “oh no I didn't put on any lipstick!” I am usually not seen without it!! I wear lipstick when I go to get the mail!

Before we left the house, I heard someone say, “possible stroke.” The word stroke didn’t register. My daughter had remembered my TIA diagnosis from back in May, but I did not! We finally went outside, and I walked to the ambulance. I was so nervous and kept talking about everything under the sun, especially the fact that I had on no lipstick or socks!

In the ER, I was sent immediately for a CAT Scan. How could I have had a stroke? My lips were still regular, I spoke clearly. I was even joking about not having dressed properly. I was a nervous wreck; but in denial about the fact that my spicy, salty, high fat diet could be the underlying cause of what I was experiencing.

“Oh Lord, there is a virus and Beryl won't be able to stay in the ER!” I thought. And I thought of all the people who had gone into ERs but never came home. I was remembering the news clips of the morgue trucks outside of hospitals! I could hear Beryl trying to bargain to stay with me. I began to think of who will be able to speak to her.

Thank God, Beryl finally left the ER on her own accord. This was the first day.

I was in the ER for hours and finally received the dreaded news, I was being admitted! What about Covid 19? Vanity visited again, as I thought about my lack of lipstick, no lotion either! It had never occurred to me that I would be admitted to the hospital!

On the 2nd Day, I was placed in a corner on the 3rd floor, with a makeshift partition for privacy. This was because the hospital was full to capacity due to the Pandemic. They were monitoring my blood pressure as it was soaring high, 400 over 100 something! I have never had a blood pressure reading so high! By now I was I was so hungry and asked for something to eat. To my surprise, I was given a real roasted turkey sandwich, on wheat bread, a small bowl of fruit, and cranberry juice, my choice.

My night was uneventful, except for the constant blood pressure checking and no television! Oh, and I had to walk down the hall, escorted, to a restroom.

Before midnight I was taken to a single room around the corner that had a huge television, but no restroom. Because I could walk, they tested my ability to hold the railing that was attached to the wall. This test I passed, but I wanted to go home.

By God's grace, my strength and balance returned. More tests and questions about mobility. Buzzes, Beeps, Bells! O my Lord, so many noises! “CODE BLUE! CODE BLUE!”, heard twice in one hour!

And now it hit me again that I had brought no toiletries and I was in need of a shower! I didn't and don't try to bargain with God, with Him, I don't play. Here is some of a prayer that I said: “Lord please, I want to go home!”

I made up in my mind that I would eat cleaner. I did and do want to be healed. I knew within my heart that God would make a way!

And guess what? HE DID, FOR I WAS DISCHARGED FROM THE HOSPITAL ON THE 3RD DAY!

On Friday December 18, 2020, I was officially discharged!

This experience has given me a new lease on life. Not to sound like a cliche, but I want to live so God can use me. In this season I am an author and an artist, filled with so much JOY! I am so grateful for all HE has done. This story is only the beginning of more of His works to come!

Finding Love at Fifty

By Leslie A. Anderson

Finding Love at Fifty

Leslie A. Anderson

My 50th birthday was a challenging time for me.

A few months earlier, a relationship ended with a man I thought I would spend the rest of my life with. When we met, I allowed myself to be vulnerable, open to love, and open to the real and distinct possibility that we would spend the rest of our lives together. It hit me like a ton of bricks when he shared with me that he didn't see a future for us, that he wasn't happy, and that he wanted the relationship to be over.

I am thinking that, professionally, I got my ish together. I am a senior executive in state government and well-respected in political and professional circles. I am managing millions of dollars, as well as managing an effective staff. Here I was now working on the part of my life that I so wanted to get together – the part about who I would spend the rest of life with or if I would ever find that someone special.

Up until this point there had been a few fits and starts with relationships that never panned out. A lot of my friends and family always indicated to me that I was too much, that I needed to diminish my shine just a little bit. "Your personality intimidates men, and you should just roll it back a bit.", they said. I was never comfortable with being with anybody, whether it was a friend or someone I was in a relationship with, who required that I diminish who I am to make them more comfortable about who they are.

Fifty is a milestone birthday for a number of reasons. You hit that half century mark and you have, so you think, more life behind you than is ahead of you. It was a time of sadness for me; it was a time of depression and it was time I didn't want to celebrate. I didn't really share my feelings with anyone I didn't let anyone in, and I didn't seek any professional help to address these issues.

I didn't stay in that place for very long. I began to look introspectively to see what I could have done differently. I yearned to discover the things that I could do to fulfill God's plan for my life because I do believe that God's hand is always in your life. But what always gnawed at me was this status quo that you can have many accomplishments yet, as a woman, you're not successful unless you're married with children or you're in a romantic relationship.

Unknowingly friends have said that to me and diminished my accomplishments – "Oh, that's great that you got this award and that's great that you invested millions of dollars that leverage billions of dollars, but you know what girl, you're not married... you know what girl, you don't have anybody in your life." That kind of noise lives in your sub-conscious and a part of you begins to believe that that you're not a complete woman unless your life is filled with the things that society suggests make you whole.

So, I looked internally. I wondered about things that I could do to improve myself. I also learned that you can't change people, you can only change how you can react and respond.

I worked for several years helping high school students go to college. A part of the curriculum was to help them understand who they are. What I came to understand was that as confident as I was facing the world, I wasn't being honest with myself about who I was.

What I needed to do was to come to terms not with who my friends wanted me to be, not with who the world wanted me to be, but with who I wanted to be.

I spent a lot of time soul searching.

I have eight godchildren who mean the absolute world to me and they are my joy. In this period of depression, they were my saving grace.

My youngest godchild wanted me to watch the movie *Maleficent* with her. I really didn't want to because I'm like "leave the Disney fairy tales alone." I thought that it was dark and creepy. Angelina Jolie's character was frightening to me. I'm a little scaredy cat; but, this godchild came over and convinced me to watch it.

By the end of the movie, I knew God was speaking to me through her. I learned that love's true kiss was not through the Prince, but the GODMOTHER. This was profound because I became a godmother when I was 16 years old. I didn't know anything about love, I was 16. No matter what happened, that little person, my godchild, loved in a way that touched me to the core of my being. This was really the love that I had been looking for my whole life. I had ignored it because I was chasing love from society's vantage point, allowing it to dictate my perception of what true love was supposed to be. It was profound and to accept it and to understand it freed me to finally focus on where I needed to be.

There was a freedom that I began to experience that I never had in my life before, I let go of the things that were truly holding me back because— (1) I knew who I was, (2) I knew what I wanted and (3) I had a new sense of peace. It was this cultivated love for these eight special people in my life who pulled me out of the darkness into the light, joy, and peace. Two years and 6 months after my 50th birthday, I celebrated my 50th birthday.

It was a celebration of life, love, and legacy. I shared my celebration that night with my mother and my self-proclaimed godmother who were celebrating 50 years of friendship. I paused to recognize their friendship because what this period of darkness also taught me was to shine the light on those that you love, to give more than you get, and to be less selfish.

I have learned that true love is the love of family, it's the love of friends, your sister girls (that black girl magic), it's the love of the children that your friends ask you to be the godmother of and accepting love in our lives as it comes. No longer do I allow anyone to tell me what it should look like or how it should be.

I wrap this story up by saying that living in the key of joy means knowing who you are and more importantly whose you are; allowing God to enter your life and into your heart to provide you with direction and guidance; discerning the voices in your head; and knowing that what's for you is for you.

Faith Over Fear

Suzanne L. Anderson

Faith Over Fear

By Suzanne L. Anderson

As I look back now, symptoms began to present themselves around September 2019 as I began to have difficulty digesting food. I attributed it to a severe case of acid reflux and self-medicated until the over counter meds were not giving me any relief.

In February of 2020 I saw my primary care physician (PCP) and, after describing my symptoms, she referred me to a gastroenterologist (GI), who in turn sent me for a series of tests. Two weeks before my originally scheduled upper endoscopy on March 31, 2020, COVID-19 hit New Jersey hard shutting everything down. My endoscopy was postponed until further notice. In May of 2020, the procedure was rescheduled for Friday June 19, 2020.

I can still see the look of worry on my GI doctor's face as she woke me up from my upper endoscopy. She said, "I need you to go for a cat scan tomorrow as the endoscopy appears to show a presence of cancer in the upper stomach."

I went for the cat scan on Saturday morning and by noon the doctor called to say that it is cancer and "I need you to see gynecological oncologist as I am not sure if the cancer is coming from the pelvic area to the stomach or vice versa." I was fortunate enough to get an appointment with the same gynecological oncologist who had cared for my mom when she had her bout with cancer. This doctor determined that the cancer was coming from the stomach and not the pelvic area. She recommended an oncologist that she knew and felt I would be happy with.

I met with the oncologist on June 29th and that's when things started moving at lightning speed. He let me know I was in stage 4, but it was treatable, and I'd be treated with a chemo cocktail of Oxaliplatin and Fluorouracil over a 12-week period. He scheduled an appointment for me to speak with the surgeon about putting in a port and my infusions would begin July 7. I had a very caring surgeon who installed the port on July 6 and my infusions started the next day.

I think because things moved so fast, I never really had the opportunity or allowed myself to become down or question why I have been stricken with cancer. I saw it as an opportunity to teach someone about faith through my journey.

I began sharing my diagnosis with close family and friends as I wanted to build a strong support team around me. I was met with a lot of support from everyone. These same friends and family would check on me to make sure I was OK, to make sure I didn't need anything, and they'll never know how much that meant to me as I took this journey. I created a special group in my phone which is called "faith over fear" and I would give them biweekly updates on my journey.

At my 6th infusion treatment, I got a call from my sister who wanted to know where I was sitting that morning. I stood up and looked out the window and there was my mom, my sister, and family friends holding signs. Even my dog nephew was there holding signs that said “You Got This”, “You are a Conqueror”, and “F Cancer”. Everybody who was there receiving treatment got a little inspiration from that act of kindness and I got to see how fortunate I was (and still am) to have such a great support team. The nurses that day were also touched by the display of support.

Sometimes you do not know how your journey is affecting others. I met a young lady who fed off of my energy and once said to me, “Every time I see you it’s like you have this glow around you and I get inspired just by seeing you, you're helping me get through this.” Faith over Fear!

in December 2020, I finished my 12th treatment and had another CAT scan and it still showed some thickening of the stomach lining. I met with the oncologist in January, and he removed Oxaliplatin from my treatment and continued with the Fluorouracil for another six treatments and then we would repeat the cat scan.

I went for another CAT scan on March 24th. The oncologist shared that my tumor markers have leveled out, so it was hard for him to see how much cancer remained in my system. “I need you to have a PET CT scan. I am going to order one.” he said to me. His previous attempts at a PET CT scan had been denied by my insurance company. I sent out a message in my Faith over Fear Group letting them know what was going on.

And they all said, we're praying that this time it is approved. I spoke to my good friend, Gail, after she received my message and she shared that I should not worry about this, but to just throw it up to God and let Him handle it. I did just that. The next morning, I received a call that the PET CT scan had been approved. Faith...and the power of God. I am claiming that the PET CT scan will show complete healing.

In closing, I have to add a very special shout out to my sister, Leslie, who has walked with me every step of the way throughout this journey.... having her by my side made it much easier. Her presence helped to sustain my joy.

Now Faith is the substance of things hoped for,
the evidence of things not seen.—Hebrews 11:1.

GOODBYE GRIEF

By Elder Janice Bennett

"...They who sow in tears shall reap with joyful singing
He who goes back and forth weeping, carrying his bag of seed
[for planting], Will indeed come again with a shout of joy,
bringing his sheaves with him"
(Psalms 126:5-6 Amp)

GOODBYE GRIEF

By Elder Janice Bennett

When we hear the word "grief" it immediately conjures up memories of loss. It sometimes reminds us that though out of sight, some thing or some feeling is still not out of mind. We not only grieve the loss of loved ones, but we also grieve the loss of dreams and opportunities. No matter what and no matter who, grief will be accompanied by regret and remorse of things we wish we had done or said.

Then there's joy. The two are diametrically different. Or are they? Could I really experience joy in the midst of pain and sorrow? God had to show me and teach me about this. It has become a journey involving a willingness to let go of a paralyzing sadness and learning to take deliberate steps toward the joy of the Lord and embracing it, which He says is my strength.

Grief can be like a visitor who comes and sometimes won't leave. It overstays its welcome, pops up unannounced. Grief sits on the front porch of your soul just waiting for a crack in the door of your will, your mind, and your emotions. If allowed, it can wreak havoc on that which you have labored so hard to control. It competes with faith and joy,

Grief is a universal experience. Every person, regardless of creed and color, will meet with it at some time or another in this life.

Academia will tell you there are five stages of grief: Denial, Anger, Bargaining, Depression and Acceptance. Like an arcade game, grief will have you feeling caught, like a pin ball, as you bounce between each of them. You think they are linear, but oh no. You will think you're at acceptance one day and then the next day you'll tell yourself, "this didn't happen." Literally. Like the pin ball, when you fall into that void, it can be only moments before you are propelled by a thrust beyond your control and you land somewhere in one of the other stages, wondering if it will ever end.

Joy, as I long defined it, was circumstance driven and thus emotionally driven. I equated it with an exuberance that bubbled endlessly. That it looked like a smile, and lightness in your step. Nowhere in my definition of joy was there room for feeling of grief. They couldn't occupy the same space! I was being asked to choose one or the other and I couldn't. If I allowed joy it meant I was unfaithful to the memory I was grieving over.

Eventually, I learned that joy is what I could embrace by faith. No matter the circumstances, no matter my emotions. And guess what? It indeed could be had in the midst of my time of grief. What I had to decide was would I allow grief to manage me, or would I manage my grief.

God intended for me to say goodbye to grief, not because it was gone, but because He promised me joy in the midst of it. He knew I would sow in tears. The tears became seed to the next moments and the next days that I thought I would never make it through.

Grief had me tongue tied, literally. I never thought I would sing again, pray again, praise again, or write again. I had to say goodbye to grief on purpose and with purpose. It got to the point that I was either going to believe God, or not. If I chose not to believe, then I was destined to a life of such debilitating pain and sorrow. I knew I wouldn't be able to live in that life, nor would I be able to fulfill the purposes and destiny God had for me. This was not an easy assignment, but one, nonetheless.

So every day I had to choose joy on purpose. I had to believe I had it by faith. I had to believe that indeed, "the joy of the Lord is my strength." And that they who sow in tears shall reap with joy in singing.

Did it happen all at once? No. Did it take a while for my emotions to catch up? Yes. But I also have become more adept at recognizing that grief is not anti-God. He created this emotion in us. After all, Jesus wept at the death of his friend,

Lazarus. However, He didn't allow it to hinder His assignment, not just in raising Lazarus from the dead, but it was one thing He needed to do on the way to the cross. It is here that I can find my joy, at the foot of the cross.

Joy isn't always exuberance or a smile. Joy is a knowing that though they may be gone from our sight, we can rejoice for the time we had with them. We can get joy out of the privilege of knowing them and thanking God that He saw fit to let us have them in our lives.

Joy has led me to a new life in a different place, geographically and spiritually. My relationship with God has deepened. I laugh with reckless abandon. I have determined to do "it" now and not later. When I look at pictures, there still remains that "punch in the gut" feeling, but it no longer stops me from believing that I have joy unspeakable.

So Goodbye Grief. I manage you; you no longer manage me.

My friend, Crystal McElrath, wrote a piece when she experienced the devastating loss of her dad. It has served me well in my journey in the key of joy. In essence it describes a man who did not live in a place of inertia but determined that no matter what lies ahead, "I'd rather die going, than just sitting here."

I wish you all the joy He has to offer.

My Favorite Fruit

By Beverly V. Brandon-Simms

My Favorite Fruit

By Beverly V. Brandon-Simms

I love fruit; I keep it with me all day long. My passion for fruit started one day while I was driving to work. I was feeling down. I needed something constant in my life; something that would keep me in a state of tranquility no matter what.

Here I was almost 50 years old, married nearly 24 years and a mother for 21 years. A blessing--yes. However, there was something not right; I felt like nothing was going as I planned for me, me and my husband, or our family. My husband and I did not click the same; the spark and fun was gone. The boys were in that "in between" stage of claiming adulthood, but still full dependents. The things they began to do, or not do, did not jive with *my* hopes and dreams for them. I felt empty, lonely and a little upset that I had devoted so much time to my family, yet they only paid attention to me when they needed something.

I was always busy at work and church, but home was becoming very different. A house is not always a home, and I was feeling this. I felt lost. I knew God was with me, but I needed rejuvenation. I needed to come out of this funk. I needed to stop going through the motions and feeling like a stranger within my own gates.

The Lord heard my cry. One day in the car on the way to work, I heard a sermon on the radio. The speaker spoke of the Holy Spirit as the Comforter. Ever so softly, I felt a calm, a sense of relief. I knew I needed to study this subject more. I needed to maintain this spirit of peace.

Every day I prayed for more and more inspiration. Soon after, I began a study of "The Fruit of the Spirit." Sure, I could quote the virtues of the "Fruit" by memory, but I had not truly experienced it in its fullness. This study was the beginning of a life change for me. I learned that so often we equate the characteristics of Fruit of the Spirit with emotions, which can fluctuate at any time. We can be up one minute, down the next. I learned that these virtues are not based upon our feelings, but rather our state of being in various situations.

This was just the "Word" I needed. I began to incorporate these characteristics in my life and a change came upon me. This is why I now keep a fruit basket full of love, joy, peace, longsuffering, kindness, goodness, faithfulness, gentleness, and self-control with me. In other words, I pray for the "Fruit of the Spirit" to dwell with me daily. I need them all, but it is something special about joy. It tastes so sweet and keeps me smiling.

Many associate joy with happiness and good feelings, but happiness is an emotion; joy is how we maintain a degree of happiness no matter what happens. Inward joy is steady if we trust God; happiness is unpredictable. Inward joy defeats discouragement; happiness covers it up. Inward joy is lasting; happiness is temporary. This was deep.

This change did not happen overnight, but slowly each day my attitude changed. Internally, I was happier. The Spirit of the Lord was living through me. The more I woke up each morning asking the Lord for the sweet Spirit of peace and joy, the brighter my days became, and I no longer relied on others to make me happy.

Soon I realized that my joy had been based on self-centeredness. I was sad and disappointed when things were not as I thought they should be or wanted them to be. I had to learn: *"Therefore, if anyone is in Christ, he is a new creation; old things have passed away; behold, all things have become new." (2 Cor.5:17, NKJV).* I had to learn that when I began to live in sync with God, I saw things differently and I could begin to rejoice in the goodness of God. The Lord gave me joy.

Did circumstances change radically? No, not right away. However, it was clear my new attitude created a more positive environment. I continued to focus on God and His goodness; I kept focusing on my blessings. Soon my feelings of being unimportant, alone, and not truly cared about faded away. The devil is always trying to throw bad pitches in my life, but daily walking in the Spirit has made me sensitive to God and His guidance through the Holy Spirit. I realize that God's love shines so much more in the midst my lows; therefore, I have no problem calling on the Holy Spirit to rain down on me to give me the comfort and guidance I need. There are too many blessings to more than cover the clouds in my life. I have chosen to look at each moment as a moment in which to be thankful. Joyfulness is my response to God's love and care for me. This joy has resulted in a higher state of peace in my life. The more joyful I am, the more at peace I am.

No matter what we are going through, we can have joy when we focus on what Jesus has done for us and what He has promised us. I reminisce on how He brought me through those times when I thought I would never make it. Please know that it is not over until God makes that decision. Nothing is final until God says it is. And, when it is, Jesus has promised me a home over there....

How can we maintain joy amidst our troubles? Romans 5 reads that we have peace with God because we are justified by faith through Jesus Christ and the access He has given us through grace. Joy is a gift from God. It does not depend upon circumstances but rather is found in Jesus' unchanging character and promises. It enables us to find hope and peace—even when life seemingly falls apart. We can rejoice in tribulations knowing that they worketh patience which produces character which produces hope. Because Jesus

Christ died for us to justify us through the blood, we have more than enough reason to be "Living in The Key of Joy!"

Afternote:

This journey that God travelled with me, was preparing me for better things. I always loved working in the church and serving the Lord. But this took on another meaning when I was ordained as an elder. The title is not important, but the extra layer of service that comes with this position is. Focusing on others and encouraging them to be joyful adds so much to my life. My daily prayer is to leave a positive spirit with all in whom I come in contact—whether it is a kiss, hug, listening ear, pat on the back, whatever. God has truly blessed me, and I want to bless others.

"These things I have spoken unto you, that in me ye might have peace. In the world ye shall have tribulation: but be of good cheer, I have overcome the world." (John 16:33, KJV)

"May the God of hope fill you with all joy and peace as you trust in Him, so that you may overflow with hope by the power of the Holy Spirit. (Romans 15:13, NIV)

Relentless Faith

By Clover Charles

Relentless Faith

By Clover Charles

The three-hour trip to the airport was uneventful and I walked to the airport check-in counter all smiles. I had accepted the opportunity to speak at a conference in Dubai. The ticket agent took our passports for check in, I looked at my husband all giddy like, but the words that followed would be ones to test my willpower.

“Where’s your visa for the Emirates ma’am?" she asked.

"Excuse me," I said, "what visa? I'm hearing you correctly?"

“Yes, you need a visa to travel to Dubai.”

“Oh my goodness, I didn't know that, can I just pay you more for it? Our flight leaves in three hours.”

“No”, she said “you have to apply online, and it takes days to acquire.”

This really can't be happening to me right now, I thought, but it was. My once in-a-lifetime opportunity was being cut short before it began.

I stepped aside and called the hotel in Dubai, only to have salt poured into my wound. It was reiterated that, yes, it took days to acquire a Visitor Visa and I was further informed that it was currently Ramadan so government offices were working half days so it would be really hard to acquire my Visa. How ironic that my speech was going to be on relentless faith and now I was faced with a seemingly impossible task.

The paperwork required for the Visa was daunting, but I wasn't going to give up. To add fuel to an already flammable situation, there were no available hotel rooms in the area near the airport, a big convention was in town. Well, I thought, at least the airport had security so sleeping at the airport wouldn't be so bad. What a misguided decision that was, ouch!

By this time my husband was a bit disgruntled, but at least he was hanging with me. I told him I just couldn't shake the feeling that I was supposed to make it to this conference. One would think that after the last few occurrences of having our flight rebooked and having nowhere to stay, that my sound decision making would've kicked in. What a battle but I refused to give in and ride three hours back home without accomplishing what I set out to do. Sure, it would have been easier to give up, but I believed that my faith could move mountains.

In the meantime, I needed a shower and a bed. It had been almost 48 hours since my ordeal began and there was still no end in sight. I thought I could budge an inch and get a hostel or something. We found a place about 20 minutes from the airport, and I could feel my eyes getting heavy. But first I had to place another call and send another email about the Visa before calling it a night. I couldn't sleep well anyway, all I could hear in my mind was, "when will you give up, can't you see you're delusional? Just go back home, you've had your flight changed twice already. What a travesty."

I finally dozed off and woke up to find out the name of the city I was in was, Chantilly. It sounded so beautiful, and the day was absolutely lovely! When everything around me seemed like it was falling apart, I still had a prayer so that's what I did. I took a walk and I prayed.

"Lord it's me, I'm leaning on your word and I have a tiny measure of faith left. If I don't get approved today, I can't make this trip because my flight will take almost 24 hours. Two days of my hotel stay have already been lost, I am only booked for five. Show up for me as you always do, Amen."

Somehow, the walk back to the lodging was so serene. I was more focused on the beauty of God's creation than the situation I was in. My husband and I got back with just enough time to grab our luggage, jump into a cab, and head back to the airport. This time I knew for sure I would be boarding a plane. "Faith is now", I kept reminding myself.

Almost 72 hours after I first arrived at the airport, I was back for the third time. I found a seat near where I could see a little bird feeding on crumbs. He seemed so content and, in some strange way, that brought me comfort, it brought me back to a peaceful place. Peace in the midst of turmoil is a real thing.

Relentlessly, I showed up in this situation and I never stopped believing I was going to make this trip, no matter how foolish it may have seemed to others. As the bird, whose presence I had found comfort in, chirped on happily nearby, I chose to remember the raven at the brook in the Bible, and remembered that my heavenly father is faithful.

The next thing I knew, I was at the airline counter with an email that said "they have approved your Visa!" As the ticket agent printed my boarding pass to Dxb International I wondered if I had accepted the first “no”, would I have known there was a “yes” waiting for me. Even days later, I expected victory and I received it but, truthfully, the stand was not easy.

After my last two and half days, going through the dreaded airport security screening was a breeze. I found my assigned seat and when I heard the voice over the intercom of the plane welcoming us to our flight, I finally shed a tear, but it was one of triumph.

Landing in Dubai and seeing the glorious architecture was surreal, and even more so was the fact that what was supposed to be a trip taking less than 24 hours took me over 72 hours due to one curve ball after another. But I made it.

As I was reminiscing, I came to the realization that I was able to turn that curve ball into something that came back around to serve me because at the conference I was able to speak so confidently on my topic after my ordeal. I rocked my speech on "Relentless Faith"! I chose to be propelled by my situation and not be destroyed by it, and at that thought the sparkle of joy that hit my heart was explosive!

This is an event I will never ever forget because when I was walking through the valley of disappointment, I chose to never stop walking. I learned you truly have to walk out the roads life carves for you. If tired rest if you must, but don't ever give up.

In closing, remember life is a journey, and on that journey we come across valleys so low and mountains so high that they may seem impassable. But, on the way through whatever situation you face, don't forget to take time to smell the flowers, embrace the sounds of the sparkling brooks, and take in the beauty of the birds' song. No matter where you find yourself, each and every bit of scenery has a purpose and, though it may seem dreary at times, if you hold on and hold out long enough, I can assure you that situation will bring you sparkles of Joy.

My Perfect Example

By Gail Clanton

My Perfect Example

By Gail Clanton

I was once asked to write an article about the empowered woman and Black Girl Magic, and I chose to concentrate on women of a "certain age." More specifically, I spoke with women who were over the age of 80. You see, I knew that they held a special brand of wisdom that could help and inspire younger generations and I wanted to tap into it.

The women that I chose to speak with didn't fail me, not one bit. I asked them what kept them going and what kept them "keeping on." In other words, I wanted to know what kept their joy intact. Here's a short synopsis of what they told me...

Woman #1 said: "I'm 88 years old. My family is what keeps me going. They care for me, I care for them, there's a lot of love between us. I try to keep myself healthy so I'm here to see them all reach their levels of success."

Woman #2 said: "I'm 84 years old. God keeps me together. I talk to Him every day. I know He's looking out for me."

Woman #3 said: "I'm 89 years old. My history motivates me to keep on keeping on. No turning back, I participated in too many marches to stop moving now."

Woman #4 said: "I am 81 years old. I keep my own self going. I know I want to live long, like my mother did, so I do what I need to do. I eat right and treat people right."

My wonderful mother is the perfect combination of all four of these women

In fact, these are all things she's said to me over the years. Her God, family, history, and her own internal sparkle are what is keeping her going... and going... and going.

Affectionately, and with much respect, I call my mother Jonesy. (I gave her this name during one Christmas season about 25 years ago, it's a long story.) She is the perfect combination of grace, wisdom, beauty, strength, and spunk and I get a great amount of pride and joy from being her daughter.

My childhood memories of my mother include funny things she said, comforting acts she performed, and the steadfast way she worked hard to ensure that my brother and I had the best childhoods possible. She partnered with my father to ensure that we always felt safe, secure, important, and loved. We had amazing opportunities, many of which our peers weren't fortunate enough to enjoy. We traveled to places far and near and we were able to receive a quality education. Yes, my brother and I were very blessed.

And did I mention that my mother is gorgeous? As a young girl I remember thinking that I had the most beautiful mother in the world. I still do. I can remember wishing that I looked more like her. I still do.

While others had to search for a role model, I lived with mine

Right before me was the perfect example to follow, so I never had to look far to find what a good, honest, caring, dedicated woman looked like. She instilled within me my love of music, shopping, theater, jewelry, and so much more. We talk often and laugh often, she makes life interesting and fun.

When my father passed away, I did what Luther sings in the song, "Dance With My Father." I cried for my mother even more than I cried for myself. My father's death was so sudden, I wasn't sure how my mother would fare. But it shouldn't have surprised me when she exemplified a strength that was second to none. She knew that her life had to go on and that there were still things for her to accomplish. She made it clear, even in the midst of her sorrow, that her sparkle was intact, thus providing an easier path for me as I journeyed through my own healing. That was a gift she gave to me when I needed it most.

One of the many things I admire most about my mother is the way she refuses to let too many things bother her. While I worry and overthink and then worry some more, my mother's more laid-back attitude and demeanor are qualities that I envy and deeply respect. She cares, and she cares quite a lot, but she's just so cool about it! Jonesy tells you what she thinks, helps you draw your own conclusions, and then goes back to her own regularly scheduled program. In other words, she deals with the issue and then lets it go. I can't help but think that this is partly why she's enjoyed such a long, beautiful, and healthy life. God has been good to her and she has adopted the mantra, "Don't Worry, Be Happy!"

Today Jonesy is an Ipad toting, piano playing, Hulu and Netflix programming, driving around town, telling it like it is, computer savvy expert who will not hesitate to let you know that she's still "got it". Please don't help her unless she asks for it and please don't underestimate her ability to get the job done.

She maintains leadership positions in various organizations and is often consulted when help is needed. Yeah, my Jonesy is the bomb!

Hanging out with my mother is one of my favorite things to do. We get along fine until we're in the car and I get lost! Then we "argue" about which way to turn and where we went wrong. But once I'm back on the right path, all is well again.

And, come to think of it, keeping me on the “right path” is something my mother has done all of my life. Through her careful teachings and loving examples, she has helped me navigate through the “highways and byways of life”, as the good church folks say, and I am grateful.

It is on the shoulders of women like my mother that trails are now being blazed by powerful women of more recent generations…

Oprah Winfrey is one of richest people in the world. Astronaut Mae Jemison has literally gone where few have ever been. And Senator Kamala Harris is Vice President of the United States.

Black girl magic is nothing new; in fact women of all shades have been magical for generations.

My mother is MAGICAL! I will forever be grateful to God for assigning her to me. My hope is that the longer I hang out with her, and the more closely I pay attention to her, a little of her magic, grace, and charm will rub off on me. For me, that will be pure joy.

Joy from Pain

By Erica Courtland

Joy from Pain

By Erica Courtland

Ten women working hard on life's field of dreams. One is called away by Endometriosis. The others keep working. The precious one called by this condition would benefit by refusing her endowment to stay in the field. It's no privilege having Endometriosis.

Endometriosis presents itself with abdominal punches, aches and jabs month by month, year after year, relentlessly causing diverse compounding damage to the reproductive organs of the afflicted. It isn't a respected diagnosis. It's difficult for men and unencumbered women to accept the severity or existence of it. It is not a death sentence, but it provides a prognosis of lifelong physical agony coupled with shameful insults and possible infertility.

My mom was excited for me to get my period. She bought a Kotex training box in 1969. Being her only girl, I guess I was supposed to feel special that only I, in the midst of three brothers, would be able to bear young in my belly.

It wasn't something I looked forward to. The Bible was clear. God's "pain in childbirth" sentence allowed Eve's apple incident to ruin the joy of childbirth for countless women, including me. Hard to get excited about painfully producing a little animal who I'd be charged to nurture for 18 years and beyond.

Even if I chose not to exercise my right to bear young, there was no opting out of the PERIOD, a monthly shedding of the endometrium. The bloody process wasn't for me. The unwieldy equipment, a crotch hammock with a belt, was awkward for a small built girl. I didn't even try to be happy about the advent of menses even though the kit was a cheery pastel color with samples and an instruction manual.

My displeasure didn't stop my body from transitioning from a tomboy into an adolescent girl. I'm guessing hormonal shifts infected my brain with crazy hopes and wild dreams. Like other wide-eyed young women, I imagined possible careers, love relationships and even children. My period was a necessary evil that wasn't so bad at first.

Eventually, my body launched a vicious attack on itself. The perpetrator was Endometriosis which my mother guardedly introduced me to during my menstruation training. I'm sure she hoped I wouldn't suffer with the condition that caused her a life of physical grief and major surgery. If you don't tell a girl about menstruation cramps, she won't imagine she has them, right?

When it hit me, I wondered what I did to deserve added discomfort to an already heinous process. Excruciating pain without childbirth! I didn't read that part in the curse of Eve. No amount of prayer or Holy Water released my monthly torture. Mom used straight bourbon. She applied hot water bottles or heating pads to my outside while the whiskey warmed my inside. That eased the pain. It actually knocked me out until I forgot I was in a world of pain.

Mom taught me many self-care tips to prepare me for leaving the nest to attend college. The most valuable advice dealt with maintaining emotional strength in the Endometriosis battle.

1. People don't care how sick you are.
2. Doctors don't know everything.
3. When you feel your worst, look your best.
4. Medication over-prescribed can be the devil.
5. Be an informed, fierce advocate for yourself.
6. Endometriosis pain is real. And,
7. Endometriosis grows on whatever body part it attaches itself to, like kudzu grows on a southern pine tree.

Managing my condition was simplified when I used birth control pills to allow fewer periods. Pregnancy was another state of remission. Yet, I had two emergency room visits when nothing but narcotics could calm my abdominal eruption.

The ER doctor insisted I probably did not have Endometriosis. He prescribed drugs and sent me away. Two years later, when we met in the ER again, he was less resolute in his opinion. He was like most doctors I consulted in my twenties. One insisted I had a psychological mishap that convinced me I was a unicorn in a fantasy pain world.

At 37, I was finally diagnosed with Endometriosis. It caused the unbearably painful enlarged ovary that was interfering with my left leg's ability to flex at the hip. A photo of my white ovary speckled in chocolate cysts was proof my suffering was real.

Hysterectomy was the expedient option. Oddly, I waxed nostalgic. It was sad losing my womb which served me well four times. However, her torment had lasted long enough. Bye uterus! Bye ovary! No more periods. No pain. No Endometriosis! Hello Menopause!

While I anxiously anticipated the major surgery to end my Endometriosis nightmare and restore the functionality of my left leg, I did a happy dance on my one good leg, focused on how blessed I was to have had children. Nearly thirty years of suffering was ending on an operating table. Merry Christmas.

I woke up from the surgery in the expected pain. Doc used my C-section scar. Very efficient. He described the large number of growths he removed hoping he excised it all.

Why had I waited so long? I hadn't waited. Doctors brushed me aside minimizing my complaints. Some insinuated I conjured symptoms of a mythical ailment that old wives told feeble minded women to use to get sympathy.

My surgeon said I could go home after I passed food. My colon wouldn't pass food. A nasal tube pumped my stomach wastes out. A tube fed me in my arm. There were no gas bubbles. No movement. What did I have to do to get moving? Literally. God told me to trust Him. It wasn't my time to see Him.

I sang the songs of Zion with urgent intent in a richer voice. How great my joy! I recalled Bible verses and forgave Eve for the accursed apple episode. A few times, I saw joy come in the morning after weeping all night. The joy of the Lord became my strength more than ever before. I passed gas and then passed food. Hallelujah!

It has been over twenty years since that Christmas of Joy. My children gradually left the nest. They've provided thirteen grandchildren who are remarkable in their intellect, athleticism and scholarship. I am thankful for every experience with them.

Mom, my traveling partner and main advocate when my marriage ended, has transitioned to Heaven. She lived a long full life in spite of her health struggles. I appreciate our relationship.

My tedious journey continues. Endometriosis is back as deep but manageable pain. I am grateful none of my daughters suffered and pray my granddaughters are spared.

I joined an online community of women with Endometriosis. The vast number of them are very young, signaling some advances in diagnosis and treatment. The frustration they express with doctors', even gynecologists', attitudes as well as limited treatment options is exasperating.

Some lack supportive systems to assist them when flare ups occur or post-surgery. Too many distraught women end their pain by suicide.

I applaud the women who administrate the forums for Endometriosis discussions. They also hold the medical community accountable for advancing treatment options. I pray my tips and testimony help bring joy out of desperation for even one Endometriosis survivor.

Endometriosis has taught me these valuable lessons:

1. Never take any day, or moment, for granted.
2. Be thankful for gas bubbles. They make babies smile.
3. Never let pain, mental or physical, interrupt my God-given joy.

Untattered

By Dr. Genevieve Cromer

Untattered

By Dr. Genevieve Cromer

The ugliness of racism, discrimination, and bias too often raises its hideous head. It pits people against one another, and it is postured on pure ignorance and fear.

My educational journey began as a young child with a mother who finished vocational school and a father who only made it to the 10th grade. My parents had insight and focused on education's trajectory power and prowess. They allowed their children to move along an educational path that sometimes meant traveling in uncharted waters.

My parents became disenchanted with the public school system's discriminative practices that did not allow black children to take books home. At that point, they decided to put their children into the Catholic school system. All seven of us graduated from the same Catholic elementary school. Five of the seven continued to Catholic high schools.

We were raised by protective parents who had suffered through racism, discrimination, and bias on several levels. My parents tried hard to shield us from the horrid past. Growing up in the southeast section of Washington, DC, our environment did not outwardly show the ugliness of racism, discrimination, and bias, partly because the percentage of black people was higher than any other group of people. This insulated cradle caused an inner thermostat without unbridled boundaries.

While in Catholic high school, I had my first taste of racism, peppered with bias, when a teacher told me that I would never graduate from one college, even though this same teacher asked if I would help my peers in that class. Nonetheless, leaning on my own resilience, I moved along unflinching. My dream of going to college was not going to be deflected by this teacher's remark because my perseverance was untattered. So much so that I only applied to two colleges. I had my heart set on going to a college in Massachusetts, and I was accepted.

My parents supported and encouraged my decision to travel to Boston, Massachusetts to continue my education. The station wagon was packed with most of my worldly possessions, homemade outfits, and off to Boston we went. Mom, Dad, and me in the cramped back seat. In that back seat, my heart was filled with a bevy of emotions, and joy was one of them. I never doubted that I would succeed!

As Daddy navigated and read the paper map, he, unbeknown to any of us, made a wrong turn. That wrong turn was my introduction and the first experience with Boston's racism, discrimination, and bias. Written on a tall building in plain sight was graffitied in big black letters that read, WE HATE

NIGGERS, WE KILL NIGGERS! We were in ominous South Boston! South Boston's white constituents gained national attention in the early seventies when they opposed desegregation and didn't want students from predominantly black communities to come to their schools. At that point, my father wanted to turn around and take me back to Washington, DC, but my mom calmed him and reassured him that his child would be safe.

I attended a small, predominantly white, all woman's Catholic college in Boston. At its inception, only affluent white women were educated there. I was often faced with racism, discrimination, and bias as the only black student in many of my classes. My welcome to Boston that first night taught me to stay close to the school and not venture out too much unless it was with a group. But as time went on and I was exposed to more racism, discrimination, bias, and imbalances, my resilience grew stronger. That unbridled nature I possessed acted as an underlining barrier.

One incident happened as I was in class and sitting the furthest away from the windows, yet my professor asked me to pass by several white women to close the windows. I remained calm and politely responded, "no." When I shared this with my mom, she was undoubtedly unnerved and afraid, but I assured her that she could stay calm. I would be OK. I also experienced challenging professors who marked my papers wrong, and I would borrow a white students' assignment to show them the comparisons. The same thing that was marked wrong on my paper would be marked right on the white student's paper. Yes, there were several irrefutable, unfairly marked essays.

In some instances, students did not want to sit next to me, the black student. This was just another sign of ignorance and racial bias. Oh, yeah, and the constant recruitment attempts to get black students to join the school's basketball team!

I moved from those situations successfully and earned a Bachelor of Science in Biology. That was my first successful college graduation.

I had decided to continue on my educational path and earn a Master's in Elementary Education. The experience at the second college was not as racially blatant as what I'd dealt with previously. Upon graduation with my Master's degree, I moved into my first-time teaching position in the Boston public school system. I was thrilled and excited to move forward.

I taught at a small, underserved, and underprivileged urban school with students from many different cultures. Again, I was awakened to realize that racism was still alive and kicking. A few of my white parents were skeptical of a black teacher and felt it imperative to sit in my class and critique my teaching. One mom sat in my classroom for days and would walk her son in on numerous occasions. My focus remained on teaching my students to the best of my ability.

Surprisingly, that white mom requested that I teach her second son, and I did. The principal would not allow her third son to be in my class, and the mom pulled her sons from our school six years before I left.

When I decided to leave the school to return to the Washington DC area, that white mother who sat in my class nine years prior stood in the school's foyer waiting to give me flowers and a note of thanks. She told me that I was the best teacher that her children had, and she wished me a successful life wherever I should go.

Upon returning to the Washington DC area and joining the Maryland school system, I found that discrimination was filtered with subtlety. My mindset remained constant in my love for learning, teaching, and sharing my knowledge with students.

I continued to move forward as I climbed the educational mountain of my chosen profession. My last course of study was all online. Remembering my past, I decided not to use my picture on my profile to avoid any racism, discrimination, or implied bias.

Reflecting on being told that I would never finish one college, I put that to rest only to permit my resilience to take me to the highest possible level of education. Completing a doctorate and surviving racism, discrimination, and bias acts along the way is a testimony to my ancestors and parents. I am proud and full of pleasure to represent them.

My faith progressed through it all and built resilience, love, and joy within me! So, to the naysayer who said that I would never graduate from one college, I have now proudly graduated from three-- untattered!

Let no one steal your joy!

"An opportunity for great joy" are times of trial that bring incredible endurance to our faith. James 1:2-4

Daily Victory

By LaVonne Dees

Daily Victory

By LaVonne Dees

Each day we are blessed to go through a variety of experiences. Some are jovial, some are not so happy. Some are etched in our minds forever, while others are soon forgotten. Some of our experiences bring painful lessons and some of these lessons are worth sharing with others.

Through all of my life experiences, I've found three things that have helped to keep my joy intact. These things are my foundation, they keep me moving forward.

The first thing is the example I was blessed to witness in the life of my Mother. My Christian Faith was established early simply by paying close attention to my Mother's words and actions. She was a woman of strength and honor.

As a small child, I watched her daily, at home and other places, and witnessed her close and interactive relationship with Abba Father, Son of God, and Holy Spirit. Memories of her smiling face and laughter continue to remind me to be joyful on both cloudy and sunny days. They also remind me to be progressive, to try new things, and to make decisions that lead to bright, happy days. What a blessing my Mom was to me and to our family.

Two years ago, I witnessed my Mom's willingness to trust God by faith as she put her hand in His hand and made her transition from Earth to Heaven. What a comfort it was to know that she was at peace.

The second thing I cling to as I try to live my days joyously is my own relationship with God. I find joy in knowing that there is a living God who knows and cares about my spoken and unspoken prayers. At age 13, I learned that I could accept this mighty Redeemer, the One who willingly died for my sins, and that I could establish my own personal relationship with Him. One of the greatest benefits of this relationship is the fact that if I ask, He will accept me as I am. I marvel daily at the fact that my Creator is just a prayer away and that He has already forgiven me for the times I have fallen short. My close relationship with the Heavenly Father is the rock of truth in my life.

I appreciate His word and I hold certain Scriptures close because, to be honest, learning to live a life filled with joy is a daily challenge. Yet, the words of the 23rd Psalm mean a lot to me. They are powerful words that I don't often hear spoken, but they comfort me. The first verse, "The Lord is my Shepherd, I shall not want" keeps me humble as I remember that He created an Earth full of food, shelter, and everything we need to sustain us and to keep us healthy. He provided for us so that we don't have to need or want for anything.

I read this Scripture and think that God must have intended for us to live as one big, happy, joyful family, one that cared for each member and kept Him at the head. We weren't supposed to be separate or divided but, sadly enough, that's exactly the way we appear to live. Separate. Divided. Not one unit at all, but scattered entities each looking out for itself.

The fact that the Earth is full of healthy soil and green foliage, makes it clear to me that we have been carefully placed on Earth. God was and is incredibly careful and selective about the way He provides for us. Verse 2 of the 23rd Psalm states, "He lay me down in green pastures. He leads me beside still water." I consider the "still water" a symbol of Him providing safety and protection from drowning and a realization that His sheep need water to drink. Because of His caring heart, the entire world has the natural resources necessary to survive, and we have a responsibility to care for these resources. Our environment was perfectly designed; it matters.

The power of forgiveness is the third thing I consider daily as I strive to keep a high level of joy. This ties in very closely with God's unconditional love and the forgiveness He's already extended toward me.

I've learned the value of keeping bonds with some people intact, while cutting ties with those who mean me no good. Some of these unhealthy friendships and relationships are just not necessary and I've learned that God can replace them with something that will bring more light and love into my life.

That said, if we are to live joyfully, we must be willing to look deep within our hearts to forgive those who have harmed us, either mentally, emotionally or even physically. Harboring bad feelings can cause damage that manifests as common health problems, accompanied by stress and anger. We have to let those friends, co-workers, associates, etc and the negative feelings associated with them go; our lives depend upon it.

We also have to forgive ourselves. There are times when we've made bad decisions pertaining to finances, dating, marriage, raising children, and the like. But, just as God has forgiven us, we must forgive ourselves.

While radio waves are not visible, they truly do exist. Similarly, we must live our lives on the right frequency so that we can tune into the Holy Spirit on a daily basis. Doing so allows us to forgive, even in the toughest situations and, in turn, brings us joy.

I believe that living in joy is our own individual responsibility. We must find examples to follow, find words to live by, and find the spiritual connection necessary to love and to forgive if we are to live a joyous life.

My daily goal is to tune into my Spiritual source and power; this could be your answer, too. It helps me to be joyous even when troubles knock on my door and allows me to spread joy to others. When I share joy through encouraging actions and deeds, I get joy in return. And, I get a mental picture of joy being victoriously spread daily – all over the world -- just as our Father intended.

Losing My Voice

By Valeria Elliott

Losing My Voice

By Valeria Elliott

It was more than a moment. It was more like a *series* of moments that led to me losing my voice.

During my childhood, my father did not talk to his children. No, he would yell at us most of the time. As a result of his behavior, at the age of five, I stopped talking. It was my way of staying out of trouble and stopping my father from yelling at me.

My father learned his behavior from his father. His father also yelled a lot so, I have to admit, my father inherited his yelling honestly. The only time my grandfather didn't yell was when he was talking to me and my siblings. We were his favorites! I think that was because we were the only grandchildren that called him Granddaddy. He would give us money almost every time he saw us.

I spent years not talking. At one point my father thought something was wrong with my hearing, so he told my mother to make an appointment to have my ears checked. He thought this might help them figure out why I wouldn't speak.

On the morning of my appointment, my father called and told my mother to put me on the phone. He told me that if nothing was wrong with my hearing, he was going to "beat my ass" when he got home. So you can imagine what that doctor's appointment was like; I didn't hear a thing! I wasn't a dumb child. The doctor gave my mom some orange medicine in a small bottle that had to be put in my ears every day, and that was that.

What my father didn't know was that I had learned how to look him right in the face, and not hear a word he was saying. I developed a mastery of ignoring him. However, eventually I think he got wind of what I was doing, so he started making me repeat back to him everything he had said.

When I stopped talking, not only did I lose my voice, but I also lost my self-confidence. On the few occasions when I would speak, there was no confidence behind my words, and I would often get cut off or talked over. Soon I convinced myself that what I had to say wasn't important. For years, people would talk over me, talk down to me, hurt my feelings, and ignore me. I allowed this behavior to go on for a long time. My self-esteem and my confidence were non-existent.

It wasn't until I gave my life to God that I got my voice back. One night, I fell on my knees and, through painful tears, I prayed and asked God to give me my voice back. God not only heard my prayer that night, but He answered it. I got my voice back, but in a not so good way.

Because of all of my years of verbal abuse, my tongue became a weapon of destruction. I would cut people up before they had a chance to open their mouths. I went from not talking at all, to telling people off in a split second. I didn't like the person I had become. I found myself praying again, this time my prayer was more specific. I prayed asking God to help me find a happy medium. He answered my prayer yet again and I got better control of my mouth. Now I'm not saying that there's not a little fire left in my mouth, but I'm much better than I was.

I thought this would be the end of the story regarding my voice. I was speaking and all was well, but God had other plans. Not only did God give me my voice back, but He told me He was going to use my voice as a Storyteller! I was shocked, how could someone like me become a Storyteller? I was hurt from years of verbal abuse. I was an introvert, shy, and I wasn't much of a people person. However, God shared with me that He had to allow me to go through those things so that He could use me to help others through the use of my stories.

God also shared with me how I had always been a Storyteller. Each time He sent someone to me to help, I would always share with them one of my stories. These stories were personal things that had happened to me and how I worked through and overcame them. God also reminded me of all the stories I made up when I was a teacher. Whenever someone needed help, my personal stories would always cheer them up. This was the reason the enemy was fighting me so hard to take my voice. He knew what God had in store for my life.

Now, I am a professional Storyteller and this brings me a lot of joy. I share my personal stories to educate, heal, free, and propel people into making new and better choices for their lives.

Into His Light

By L. Breezee Harris

Into His Light

By L. Breezee Harris

We were set up. A conspiracy was instituted many eons ago and we bear the brunt of cruel sabotage to this very day!

Growing up we read those stories that filled our heads with dreams of Prince Charming and the Knight on the White Horse. Who didn't picture themselves as Cinderella, Snow White or Sleeping Beauty? All those stories ended with the man of her dreams coming to sweep her into the blissfully, wonderful world of Happily Ever After! Sabotage!

Like so many little girls, I grew up dreaming of *my* Prince Charming, the one who would save me from my loneliness, and we'd live happily ever after. SIGH! Many, many, MANY years went by without my Prince and, at some point, I accepted I was going to live my life like one of the step sisters, no prince for me. With practice, I pushed aside my *happily ever after* dreams and faced the truth. Not everyone ended up with the knight in shining armor.

I settled into my Just-Me life and resumed my love of books. They were safe, happy escapes that filled my empty days. Until the day he broke into my safe world, and everything came crashing down.

I was engrossed in my book when a voice intruded, "It must be a really good book. I've never seen someone walk and read at the same time." (Mind you, this was well before cell phone texting, I like to think I started that trend!) I'd seen him on the train before, but never paid attention beyond that.

Let's look at this again from my point of view. I'd tried the "is he the one?" route, it did *not* work. Unless Jesus told me *personally* this was the man for me, I wasn't venturing outside of His will again. So many times I'd picked someone, *then* prayed he was the right one. God didn't make mistakes, and I was determined to wait on Him. Besides, I was finally in a place where I was good with being alone. NOPE, no thanks! I smiled, said "it's a skill" and went back to my book. But he continued talking, so I closed my book and made polite conversation until the train came in. Then I did my best to disappear.

That evening I was settled in my seat on the subway with my book when the man from the morning sat down across the aisle from me.

"I'm glad this day is over." he said. Inside I sighed, but answered "me too.", and turned back to my story. He asked me something else, I answered, and that's how it started. Over the weeks I learned about him and slowly he wore down my defenses. We began sitting together, and soon we started seeing each other.

I'll admit I was flattered that an intelligent, educated, man was singling me out. I opened the door in my heart that housed all those fairytales and dreams I'd locked away so long ago, and I allowed HOPE to float out. Suddenly my days were filled with the magic of love!

Our marriage was wonderful, we lived in this blissful bubble of joy! Until I came home from work six months after saying "I Do" and he wouldn't talk to me. I'd been so happy to get home to him, but when I hugged him he didn't respond, nothing, like I was hugging a bag of potatoes! I asked a question, and he grunted an answer. Finally, after begging him to please tell me what was wrong he snapped at me, "Nothing's wrong, except you asking me the same question over and over again! God!".

That was the first time. He seemed disgusted by my presence for the next two or three days. Then he came to me, apologizing. Some work thing had upset him, he was so sorry he took it out on me, he adored me, please forgive him.

As the years went by, the episodes increased, weeks with zero communication, as if I didn't exist. And always, at the end were the apologies, the promises and declarations. We tried counseling through our church and different medical professionals. Each time, at the end of those sessions, there'd be that promise to work to save the marriage.

Don't get me wrong, I was *not* blameless. There were things I needed to fix, too. The difference was I was willing to do the work.

After a particularly long period of silence, I was praying about what to do. I was so unhappy, and asked God to direct me. I felt the Lord say to me, "I didn't create you for pain and I don't want you to suffer. You do not have to live like this. You Do Not Have To Live Like This."

WOW! It was okay to say I deserved better! I told my husband I was tired, and ten years of trying had to come to an end. He begged me to do a new counseling session and promised to abide by all the instructions given. I agreed but confirmed this was my last effort.

After the session I felt so hopeful. He'd admitted things he'd emphatically denied in previous appointments. We agreed on the doctor's plan and promised to use the tools provided.

That evening I made a comment about our dog. He sneered and said, with derision, "you're crazy, you need professional help". I looked at him closely, trying to see if that mean person was back. He was. I tried the techniques given to us just hours earlier. He looked at me as if I disgusted him, said I was too stupid, and to leave him alone until I got some professional help. My heart sank, but I tried once again, asking him to please respond as we agreed earlier. He rolled his eyes, chuckled, and ignored me.

Looking back, I don't think I was shocked, maybe just surprised his promise hadn't lasted more than a few hours. The difference was he didn't know about my God or that I'd been given the strength and the power to overcome all obstacles! The Lord had planted my feet on solid ground, and I had no more fear.

It took me a little over a year to get myself together, find a place to live and to move. God held me in His loving embrace while I worked on building my life, one step at a time. I stumbled, and sometimes I doubted myself, but I'm happy to report I made it!

God continues to guide me and keep me safe. Every step of the way, I feel His presence and His love. Nothing I did was without His touch, and I'm so grateful He led me into His never-changing Light.

The Joy of Fellowship With My Favorite Veteran

By Irma Hinton

The Joy of Fellowship With My Favorite Veteran

By Irma Hinton

Serving my country in the United States Army and becoming a veteran are two things that I'm most proud of accomplishing and they give me great Joy. I entered the Army in 1981 at the age of 18, right after high school, because I wanted a new experience. I followed in my brother's footsteps because I knew it would be an opportunity for me to serve my country and make my own money to help my mother financially. Little did I know, the Army experience would be much more than I could ever imagine.

I was able to travel, learn new skills, and meet new people from different countries, races, backgrounds, religions and cultures. It taught me respect for myself and others, compassion, character, integrity, discipline and how to be a leader to my peers and the soldiers under my authority. I retired after 23 years of service, as a Master Chief, Personnel Sergeant, with a host of skills, experiences, and opportunities that have helped to shape me into the person I am today.
My daughter, Nichole, who is my pride and joy and my twin (she looks just like me), is also a veteran. She followed in my footsteps and entered the Army after college at the age of 23

in 2009. She served for four years and was honorably discharged as an Intelligence Specialist.

We are like two peas in a pod, we were baptized together and we both sang in the choir at our church. From hanging out with me as a little girl, riding in the car everywhere with me, Nichole knows I love old school music and listening to my 70's music. She now loves my music, but of course she takes it to a whole other level with her favorites like the Beatles, Mommas and the Pappas, Etta James, and Dorothy Dandridge. I'm more of a Temptations, Jackson Five, Stylistics, Ohio Players, Earth, Wind and Fire girl. She thinks she knows more about my kind of music than I do, yeah right. She was amazed to learn I knew all the lyrics to *Rappers Delight* by Sugar Hill Gang. Once she found out I knew all the words, she had to learn them too. Now we perform it together whenever we do karaoke.

We enjoy traveling together, too. We've taken cruises to the Bahamas, flown to South Africa, Dubai/Abu Dhabi, Egypt, Hawaii, Las Vegas, New Orleans, and taken road trips to North Carolina, Georgia, Florida, Ohio, Pennsylvania, and New Jersey. During our road trips, we enjoy visiting family, African American museums, and Civil War battleground sites. Once, for Nichole's birthday, I agreed to jump from a plane 30,000 feet in the air with a man attached to my back. It didn't dawn on me until I was falling through the sky how terrified I was. Jesus, Mary and Joseph! I was scared out of my pants jumping out that plane. I screamed through the entire free fall, my stomach went through my toes, I couldn't open my eyes because they went to the top of my skull. Who in their right mind would do something like this? You would think I would be fine with doing this being in the Army. NOT!! Let me tell you, the closest I came to jumping out of a plane was when I had to jump from a helicopter that was about 3 feet from the ground and we had to jump, roll and run into the woods, THAT'S IT! You do some crazy things for your kids.

The best part about serving in the military are the benefits you get to enjoy once you leave and become a veteran. Now that we are both veterans, it's one more thing my daughter and I can enjoy together. Being a veteran gives you an extra edge and privilege in so many areas. We get the GI bill, VA home loans, free healthcare, access to military bases, veterans preference when applying for government jobs, etc, etc. which is all good but that's not even what I want to write about. For me, being able to enjoy with my daughter all the FREE FOOD offered to veterans on Veterans Day is what brings me the most JOY.

Let me tell you how serious this is. This is so serious that we make our plans the day before. We research all the restaurants and eateries honoring veterans with free meals. We figure out which ones are close together so we can hit as many as we can without driving too far.

We start out early deciding where we want to go first, planning a time and place to meet. Our first stop is *IHOP* for a free breakfast. I mean 2 eggs, red, white and blue pancakes, bacon or sausage, hash browns. The food is so good and hot and FREE. I mean all you can say is THANK YOU JESUS!!! What a Joy. Then to *Chili's* for some chips, salsa and a delicious margarita with a nice, thick, juicy, messy quarter pound bacon cheeseburger and crispy fries, yes, yes, yes!!

We then head over to *Texas Roadhouse* for some fall-off-the-bone barbecue ribs and chicken with homemade cornbread. Once we've licked our fingers from that good barbeque, we head over to *Olive Garden* for a full meal of good old-fashioned lasagna with lots of cheese, or spaghetti with endless salad and bread sticks. I mean, cheese and crackers!! Who can turn this down? You're like a kid eating your favorite ice cream, licking your fingers and swinging your feet under the table because you're so happy. We don't usually eat the entire meals except for the breakfast meal. We normally order our food and a drink, eat a few bites and get the rest to go. This is very special for us because it's our mother/daughter quality time when we get to share, laugh, talk and fellowship with each other and we look forward to it each year.

One of our favorite restaurants to go to is *Applebee's,* for a delicious steak with sautéed onions and mushrooms, baked potato with the works and broccoli or a lime chicken and rice meal. This is our favorite because this is where we usually meet up with all the other veterans enjoying the same free meals. There's a lot of noise, fun, laughter, free cocktails and fellowship, plus war stories from other veterans. These are veterans from all the different branches of the military who served in previous wars and campaigns all over the world, including Vietnam, Iran, Iraq, Afghanistan, Kuwait, Korea and Germany. As you can guess, by now we are both so stuffed, we can hardly move but that's no reason to turn down a free meal. We keep eating, talking, drinking and laughing and having ourselves a ball. After *Applebee's*, we cross the parking lot over to *Hooters* for a basket of 10 free wings with our favorite sauce. If we feel like it, we may stop at *Krispy Kreme* or *Duncan Doughnuts* for a free doughnut before heading home.

Veterans from all over the area enjoy this day and you can feel the pride, joy and camaraderie from each of us. I love this time-honored tradition because, not only do I get to celebrate being a veteran and eat for free, but I also get to experience it with my favorite veteran, my daughter. Who could ask for anything more? I thank God every day for this wonderful feeling of Joy.

SUFFER NOT: THERE IS ANOTHER DAY

By Carol Johnson

SUFFER NOT:
THERE IS ANOTHER DAY

By Carol Johnson

The year 2020 started just like any other new year. I was living in the state of Maryland as a recent widower and a lifelong introvert. I chose to continue working to be around people and to stay busy. I considered my work colleagues, church members, and club members my extended family.

On January 6, I had in/out hip replacement surgery on my right hip. My recuperation was going well until my health support team came down with the flu. So, I returned to my home earlier than scheduled. Things were going well until three days later when I had a nasty fall that damaged my left hip, causing my sciatica to flare up. From that point, I suffered with pain morning, noon, and night! I suffered!

Prior to my fall, the Chinese authorities shut down Wuhan, a city of 11 million, due to COVID-19, which heightened the urgency for the U.S. response team to take note. Additionally, I learned of the death of Kobe Bryant, his daughter, and several other passengers due to a helicopter crash. These events started a chain of emotional rollercoasters.

Meanwhile masses of people were becoming ill, and many were dying, while others struggled to fight to overcome this corona virus. This number included many of our frontline healthcare workers. It was mid-March before we officially realized that the world was in a corona virus pandemic, and a mandatory shut-down was issued for everyone except for essential workers.

As for me, it was April before my doctors were able to prescribe a combination of medications to ease my pain enough for me to return to work (at home). However, three days after returning to work, my best friend, my mother, passed away. We were not allowed to hold a typical viewing and funeral at our home church to include my mom's family and friends due to the pandemic. My heart hurt – suffer not!

As the year progressed, racial and social unrest followed when George Floyd was unmercifully killed at the hands of the Minneapolis, MN police on May 25. The murder happened during an arrest for allegedly using a counterfeit bill, and it was viewed on national and international TV. We watched him slowly die with a policeman's knee lodged in his neck. Protesting was necessary; however, the riots and looting that followed were not. Regardless, of the negativities surrounding me, I vowed to do my best to make me and at least one other person feel happy daily with the God-given joy within me.

As we moved further into the year of 2020, there were murderous hornets spotted in the United States, shootings in

Texas, the firing of the State Department Inspector General, the death of Ruth Bader Ginsberg, and the Presidential election. With all of this and the corrupt political system in the news, I began to feel rather anxious, frustrated, isolated. Nonetheless, I was also somewhat hopeful simply because I am normally a positive person and I walk by faith. Suffer not!

I was concerned about the health and welfare of not only me, but also of my family and friends especially after finding out that one of my friend's fifteen-year-old grandson contracted the coronavirus and succumbed to his illness. I was saddened by this news; however, I was so thankful that the other two members of his family who contracted the virus survived it. I am also grateful that even when this virus hit a few of my family and friends, they were quarantined without hospitalization and they survived. Additionally, most of us still have jobs, homes, and ultimately, we are staying in place and are safe.

Although, I lost my job due to the pandemic, I am thankful I was able to retire. It gives me insurmountable joy to participate with my church members in morning prayers, Sunday School, Sunday services, Bible study, the prophetic word, and other church activities. It also gives me joy that I can still meet with my club members even though it is all done virtually.

Today, even as an introvert, it has been a little difficult for me because I miss my family and friends and have not been able to hug or kiss them since December 2019. My family and I typically celebrate everyone's birthdays and special occasions throughout the year. We are trying to do our part by staying in and staying safe. God has remained faithful and merciful.

I am learning how to embrace the comfort of solitude. By this I mean that I can appreciate the forced "slow-down" because I am finding other things to do with the extra time that I now have. Being alone is not a problem for me since I live alone anyway, but I was always glad for the opportunity to go whenever I wanted to. However, I am finding that there is peace and comfort in this solitude. I am learning new skills around the house, such as how my boiler and air conditioner function. I am doing more on my own and feel that these and other challenges are no longer a problem for me.

I have learned to decrease my anxiety level and increased patience, especially over things that I have little to no control over. I pray all day! Through prayer I can overcome almost anything. I no longer take medication for anxiety! I can look at the news and read about the issues of the world without it bothering me as before. Typically, when I now read an article or listen to the news that is disturbing, I say a prayer and move on. I have learned how to comfort my family and friends when needed. In addition, I am learning new Microsoft skills via online classes, and I am trying to develop a healthier lifestyle by eating better and exercising.

Once this pandemic is contained and we can return to some type of normalcy, the first thing I want to do is invite my granddaughter to my home. She recently graduated virtually from middle school and will soon continue her education in high school. I also want to invite my great-granddaughter over, she was recently promoted from elementary school to middle school. I look forward to visiting with them, along with their parents and siblings. I can't wait to prepare their favorite meal, a seafood boil. But before we eat, I am going to give everyone a kiss and a big bear hug.

My Pastor selected me and six other members to revamp the scholarship ministry including creating bylaws, etc. Scholarships will be for our church members and for people in the community. Even though there is a lot of work ahead, I am proud to announce that we awarded three scholarships for semester 2020/2021.

Suffer Not: There is Another Day!

I think about how God provides for us if we just have faith over fear. "Trust in the Lord with all your heart. Do not depend on your own understanding. Seek his will in all you do, and He will show you which path to take. Do not be impressed with your own wisdom. Instead, fear the Lord and turn away from evil. Then you will have healing for your body and strength for your bones." – Proverbs 3:5-8 NLT

In conclusion, my favorite quote is: “Don’t ever make decisions based on fear. Make decisions based on hope and possibility. Make decisions based on what should happen, not what shouldn’t.” – Campaign Trail in Phoenix, 2008. Michelle Obama.

The Helper Outer

By Vanessa Hall Jones

The Helper Outer

By Vanessa Hall Jones

"Good afternoon, this is the YMCA. How may I help you?", the voice on the line asked. Drawing deep breaths and rapidly replying, I asked, "Do you offer swim classes for old people? I've never swam a day in my life, and to boot, I am a Black female who fears the water. I need someone with the patience of Job."

The listener chuckled. "Yes, ma'am. We have someone for you. When would you like to start? Would you be interested in coming in and taking a tour of the pool area? We offer private lessons and group lessons. I can give you an aquatic application or you can fill out the form online."

"Oh, that would be marvelous. I'll come in tomorrow. I'm one step closer to overcoming another fear. And I think I better take private lessons." I answered.

The next day, I went to the YMCA after work with my downloaded application. Given my prior phone speech, the listener remembered me and giggled. "I'm Judy" she said. "By the end of the day, I will call you to let you know who your swimming instructor is." I thanked her and left.

Rushing to the swim outlet, I parked my car, let out a forceful sigh, clutched my handbag, and entered the store. Once inside, I made a beeline for the Athletic Department. Recalling the Olympic swimming tournaments I'd watched on television, I selected a black Speedo swimsuit.

Blue fog goggles with adjustable straps, Speedo competitive nose clips, black swimmer Speedo cap and matching earplugs all hung on the back wall. I was literally surrounded by swim gear. I lay my selections in my basket as I searched for an extra-large beach towel, poolside shoes, and a cream swimsuit lace cover-up. Given the number of garments in my caddy, I knew I would look like one of those gold medalists once I was in my swimming attire.

Soon I felt my cell phone vibrate inside my purse and I answered. "Ms. Jones, this is Judy. Jordan will be your swim instructor, and he will see you tomorrow, early Saturday morning, at seven o'clock."

"Geez, that was fast", I said. "I will see Jordan on Saturday morning. Goodbye."

My eyes gazed at the tapestry of stars on display as I peered out my bedroom window that night. My long-awaited introductory swim lesson would start in four hours and fulfill one of the many dreams on my bucket list. This was happening at the perfect time. The narrative of my divorce proceedings defined much of my time back then and had robbed me of my inner peace. I needed something different in my life.

On Saturday morning I arrived at the pool swaddled in my cream swimsuit covering. A chocolate well-defined muscular Tirhakah, King of ancient Ethiopia, stood to greet me.

"Ms. Jones?"

"That's me."

"I'm Jordan, your instructor."

"This is a kid. And muscular at that", I whispered to myself.

As we neared the kiddie pool, I told Jordan I had changed my mind. "Oh, no, you're not." he spoke.

The ancient Ethiopian king removed my cream covering, leading me to the water's edge. As I was trying to run back up the one step from the rippling waters, he clasped my hands, and we went to war. Thinking that I gripped his shoulders, my hands slithered down his water-soaked, rock-hard physique as I pulled at his swimming trunks. Jordan struggled to hold on to his swimming shorts and me at the same time. The ancient

Pharaoh cradled my hands and gingerly spoke, "You are going to be okay."

I promised Jordan that I would do better at my next lesson if he would just let me go home. He wasn't having it. Instead, he held my hands and led me closer to the kiddie pool area for beginner swimmers. Walking back and forth, he splashed the crisp waters on me and soon my first lesson was over.

"I will see you on Wednesday at six o'clock," He said.

"Lord willing, and the creek don't rise," I responded. Jordan's squinched brows and confused expression quickly let me know that he had no idea what I meant. I took a breath of relief, took a shower, and went home.

Wednesday after work, I headed to the YMCA. Jordan was waiting.

"I just finished my homework. Now, it's time for *your* classwork," Jordan said.

"Homework?"

"Yes, Ms. Vanessa. This is my last year of high school."

"Just what I thought, how is this kid going to teach a grown woman like me?" I mumbled to myself.

"Ms. Vanessa, I'm gonna need you to stop stroking that water like you're petting a cat. Dig deep and make sure you kick your legs like a shark is after you."

After each class, I practiced on my own what Jordan had assigned me to do. A lot of days, after he got out of the pool, Jordan would come back and teach me a new swimming technique for free. "You remind me of my mom. I want her to learn how to swim, but she won't" he said.

As each lesson progressed, I felt energized and noticed improvements. One day Jordan told me it was high time I learned the backstroke. Lying on the surface of the water, trembling like jelly on a rickety old table, Jordan sang gospel songs while holding my shoulders with his quite-respectable brawny hands. I mimicked the backstroke movements and was soon swimming on my own, heading toward the flag poles at the other end of the pool. On my way back to the starting point, and in the middle of the pool, I stopped, stood up, and put up my hand to ask a question.

Like a training drill sergeant, he shouted. "All questions will be answered when you reach the other end of the pool. Get going!" Rolling my eyes, I swam.

"What is your question?"

"Never mind, I made it. I was tired, and I wanted to walk back."

Laughing, he made me swim back to the flag poles and swim back to him again. The lesson ended.

A year and a half after my lessons began, I had learned how to swim. I was 50 years old and could be seen proudly strutting around as if I owned the Y's swimming pool. Freestyle, sidestroke, breaststroke, backstroke, I mastered each of them. My next goal was to learn how to do the butterfly stroke. I was still working with Jordan and one day, in the midst of me doing a dolphin kick, he stopped me. His eyes welled with tears, Jordan informed me he had joined the Navy and would be leaving in a couple of weeks. He said that he would try to find someone to continue my swim lessons. Crippled with emotions that my helper outer was leaving me to go after his dream of becoming a Navy sailor, I was indebted that the pool waters masked my watery eyes as I swam.

As a youngster, Jordan respected and supported my inability to swim. A divine intervention connected us: his yearning to teach people to swim and my desire to learn. I am so grateful that an ancient black Ethiopian king helped me to realize such joy and achieve my desire to swim.

Joy and The Southern Tour

By Dr. Katrina E. Miller

Joy and The Southern Tour

By Dr. Katrina E. Miller

One of my greatest joys is the trip I get to take with my BFF (Best Friend Forever) every year. We did not go in 2020, but that does not count because it was not a "regular" year. That year was an exception to every rule that was made, Anyway, I digress. The "Southern Tour", as we call it, was born out of our need to get away. It occurred shortly after my BFF's divorce and we wanted to hang out and do our absolute favorite thing -- shop!

As natural born planners, we decided that we would not plan anything about this trip, we only knew that it would involve shopping. This was not an easy feat. Not only did our collective and individual groups of friends look to us as the planners, but our families did also. When on a trip, we were the ones folks would ask "What are we doing today?" and we would have the answer. We were the group members who had researched the area and would map out what day would be the best to visit each site. We would know how much the admission fee was for the tourist attraction and the hours of operation. So, as you can see, going away for three or more days (we never knew how long we would be gone) without planning anything was going to be a challenge for us. Nevertheless, we were up for the undertaking.

I must admit, during the days leading up to the very first Southern Tour, we often had to tell each other "remember we aren't planning that." We did have one rule and that was that the car had to start out heading south. To ease the minds of our family, we did decide that once we checked into our hotels each night (we never knew where we would stop), we would call and let our families, or a dedicated friend, know what state we were in, the city and address of the hotel, and what time we planned to check out.

Our first year was really exciting. Since I live South of my BFF she came to my house. We left that same day with the car headed southwest. We drove about 45 minutes before we saw several of our favorite stores and decided to stop to go shopping. We also noticed during this first trip (as women over 50) we made a lot of bathroom stops. Therefore, we decided to chronical the many restrooms we stopped in. I know, sounds silly, but it made for an interesting and fun set of pictures.

I must admit we did not get very far on that day one. We shopped, went to the bathroom, shopped, stopped to eat, shopped, and then went to the bathroom again. We felt it would be against the trip gods if we did not get at least 2 hours away from my house before stopping for the night, so we drove another hour and then decided where to sleep.

Now deciding on a hotel is one of the most important parts of the Southern Tour. We usually park near a cluster of hotels and start making phone calls. Of course, besides how much is a double for the night, we would ask the night clerk such intriguing questions as “do you serve free breakfast”, “do you have a pool” (which we never used) and my favorite “do you have free cookies?” Asking these questions brought us such joy as we decided on the best rate and safest looking hotel.

We then show up in the lobby of the hotel we had selected. We are often asked by the poor soul at the desk if we had just called. Depending on which group of questions we had subjected them to, we would answer yeah or nah.

Over the course of these trips, (we have taken 4 in total), I have discovered that we can really get discounted room rates if we checked in after midnight and once even got a 2-bedroom suite for the price of a regular room. Oh, we have also been asked if we wanted one bed or two and after our initial looks of shock, (as heterosexual females), the clerk said, “I have to ask”, we became used to their selection of questions for us.

So exactly where have we ended up on these trips? Well, most of the time at a shopping center. The first year we did make it as far as Charleston, SC. My BFF had never been there so naturally this was a great place to go. We went to the market downtown and decided to have lunch. During lunch we talked about taking a tour, spending the night and visiting some of the other tourist attractions. We decided we did not want to do any of those things and headed north and back to my home. I know this may seem like a waste of time, but we honestly saw no problem with it and decided we could be back to my house in 4 hours. Therefore, we would find a local shopping center to visit and my BFF would head home, north of course, on the next day.

We have shopped in Atlanta, Clemson, and a whole lot of small towns we have never heard of. We made it to the Biltmore estates one year to see the gardens but turned around after deciding we did not want to pay the admission price. We went shopping instead. One year we traveled North. Yuck, is all I can say. We did not have as much fun, nor did we meet interesting people, AND it was expensive! But the ice cream was good. LOL!!

We have been flirted with (by males and females), met people from our hometowns, been chased by dogs (I'll keep that story to myself), ran into people we were trying to avoid, and played detective more than once. We have bought fruits and vegetables from roadside markets and asked more than one stranger "Where are we?"

I know this may not sound like much of a vacation to you, the reader, but I cannot tell you how much joy I experience during these outings. I think it might be the fact that I get to enjoy the company of someone who has seen me at my very best and at my worst and still wants to hang out with me. It might be the freedom of singing all the songs I knew as a teenager, as loud as I want in the car, and eating calorie conscious snacks at will.

It might be the fact that I have been blessed to be able to purchase all the items that I want and return them on the way back home because I later decide that I really do not like them. It may be the fact that we stop for ice cream every year at an ice cream shop in the South, and can safely purchase it. And, if we choose, we can sit down to eat it.

I also think it is the fact that my mother would have considered a trip like this to be unsafe not only for a Black female, but for Blacks in general. For all of these reasons, and so many more, just thinking about the "Southern Tour" brings a smile of joy to my face.

Heartbreak to Healing

By Yolanda Miller

Heartbreak to Healing

By Yolanda Miller

I know when you read that title you probably thought to yourself "Who broke her heart?" But did you know that heartbreak does not have to always come from a romantic relationship? A child feels heartbreak when they lose their favorite toy.

And did you know that some people don't even know they are heartbroken, they just know that they don't feel the same? That was me! I guess you wonder, how can a person not know they are heartbroken. Well, when you always push your feelings down so that you can be there for everyone else, you don't feel it. You keep moving, you keep being that emotional support for everyone else, you don't recognize your feelings, at least not at first.

I would always make people smile or laugh but then be sad on the inside. I know you are probably saying to yourself, "this is supposed to be a story of joy or happiness", but to understand the healing you have to understand the brokenness.

You see, I have always been happy. Yes, I had moments of disappointments and sadness, but I always knew why. For instance, when I was in elementary school, I participated in a pageant and lost. And there was the time when I was in college and didn't have a date for Valentine's Day. I understood the sadness in both of those instances. But in 2010, I began to wake up crying every morning not knowing why. It eventually stopped, but I was slowly changing. Even my coworkers saw the change, but I still didn't know why. People thought it was because of the weather. You see, I am from North Carolina but was then living in upstate New York. It is always cold there. Family and friends would recommend things like light therapy because they thought I wasn't getting enough sun; until almost a year later when I found myself in the bed crying for three days straight.

One day my supervisor called me and all I could do was cry on the phone. She suggested I visit a doctor and I did the very same day. Like a lot of doctors, he said, because of my job, I was depressed and prescribed an antidepressant. He never recommended therapy, just meds. I took the medication one time and felt so bad I didn't take it again. After a few weeks, I finally went to therapy. I didn't know what to say or where to begin. The therapist guided me through every word. She wanted to take me out of work, but I refused. I went back to work and completely broke down, so I had to leave. Then the therapist convinced me to take the medication again, but to ask the doctor to change the dosage. I did, then became numb. You see I was the person who always smiled and loved to see others smile. If you have ever taken an anti-depressant, you know that one of the side effects is that you can become totally emotionless.

I can remember during this time my mom decided that she was going to come check on her baby. On the inside I was so excited to see her and so thankful, I wanted to cry but I couldn't. I tried so hard, but nothing would fall. Funny, as I write this part I am crying now. I just hope my mom knew how grateful I was that she spent those three weeks with me. She even went to a counseling session with me, so she could figure out how to help me. I will never forget that. Okay, okay let me whip my face and stop crying so I can get through this story.

After about three months of counseling, I felt a little better. I stopped taking the meds because I didn't like walking around like a zombie. The counselor even helped me figure out why and when my depression started. It started when I lost my aunt in March of 2010. She was the closest person to me that represented my mom. My mom was over 700 miles away, but I could always go visit my dear Aunt Patty. We used to laugh and talk and she gave the best advice. I didn't realize how much her death affected me until I went to counseling a year later. After we figured it out, my counselor suggested that I leave Rochester, NY because she felt that I would not make it through another winter there. So, with all the paperwork filled out, my job approved a transfer and I was able to move back home. My dad flew up to help me pack up my apartment and I left October 2011 and moved back home to Rocky Point, North Carolina.

When I returned home, I just knew I would be better, but it wasn't that easy; nothing worth fighting for ever is. I was fighting for my life, I was fighting for my happiness again, I was fighting for my PEACE. But through my fighting I still smiled.

After being home and going through therapy for a year, my life again turned for the worst, just when I could kinda see the light. I lost my best friend, my heart, the one I knew would always come to my rescue while teaching me a lesson. I lost my mom. God said her assignment was complete and she gained her wings October 2012. Man, that hurt was like no other. And I fell down again; but we fall down to get back up. I was down for a good while, but I got so tired of living that way.

Then God sent me the best counselor. Have you ever met, what I call, your medical match? The medical professional that gives you right back what you give them? They force you to not to give up, they make you test your surroundings and make you take a serious look at yourself? Well, that was her. She made me take a good look at myself and she helped me identify the good people in my life. She told me the process was going to be hard because I had taught people how to love me incorrectly and I had to retrain them. I lost friends and some family looked at me differently, but that was okay. You see that process started my healing.

Wow, that was almost seven years ago. Today I am the happiest I have been in a long time. I used to have muscle spasms in my back because I carried my depression and stress in my back which caused me to miss work a lot. But I am so thankful that I have not had a muscle spasm in two years. I just moved to a new city and I am super excited to see all the new things that God has in store for me. My relationships with my family and friends are the strongest they have ever been. I am surround by supportive people and people who see things in me that I could never see; like my cousin pushing me into writing this story. This is something I probably would have never done otherwise.

I guess the moral of my story is, through your heartbreak there will be times that you will fall but don't stay there. Remember to get back up because when you take that first step toward happiness and joy, the healing process begins. LET'S KEEP HEALING TOGETHER!

A Sharecropper's Daughter

By Linda E. Owens-Little

A Sharecropper's Daughter

By Linda E. Owens-Little

Growing up on a farm in the 1950s was a wonderful experience for me…

My dad was a sharecropper. He grew tobacco and he worked on land owned by Mr. Ed. Daddy started his day at 5:30am and he worked along with his three older sons, my brothers, Junior, Lanny, and Piney. Everybody in the country had nicknames, but I'll tell you about that later.

I remember one particular morning when the sun was exceptionally hot and I couldn't sleep. I overheard Mom and Daddy saying harsh words about Mr. Ed. He was a very difficult man to work for. Mom didn't like the way he talked down to Daddy, but Daddy held back his anger and frustration because he had a family to take care of. And as he told Mom, "the only way is farming".

Mom shook her head and went back to fixing breakfast. She prepared a full breakfast on most mornings consisting of eggs, country bacon, fried potatoes with lots of onions (that's the way Daddy liked them), applesauce, fried tomatoes, link sausages, and pancakes. There were some mornings when we didn't have quite that much, but we always had something.

My mom was a good cook and she did not believe in throwing away food. For example, she used old bread to make the best tasting bread pudding ever. We never went hungry. We had the largest garden around and we ate from the earth. Mom seldom went to a grocery store for anything.

My mother, Louise, was an attractive woman. She had coal black hair, with dark brown eyes, and she loved to dress up. She often talked about her adopted family, the people who raised her. They gave her lots of love and instilled in her an understanding of how to be independent. Mom encouraged us to learn more than one skill so that we would always have something to fall back on.

On this particular morning, as I watched Daddy put on his coverall on over his clothes, I realized that as much as I admired him, I didn't know him very well. So I got up the nerve to ask him why he worked so hard on Mr. Ed's farm; why he couldn't own his own farm; and why is it that he never complained.

He replied to me, "Baby girl, one day I plan to own a farm, but right now I got to do what I can to keep a roof over our heads." I nodded. I understood.

To work the farm, I think you had to love long hours and hard work. My older brothers helped Daddy most of the time during the summer, while school was closed. Most of my brothers disliked farming, especially my brother Junior. As soon as he turned 18 years old, off he went and found a job as an auto mechanic. But my brothers Lanny, Piney, and Daddy were inseparable. All of them up at the crack of dawn and down with the sun.

Daddy harvested 24 acres of tobacco land in rural Southern Maryland. He worked on Mr. Ed's farm for ten years before we left for a new farm.

The house on the new farm was great! Mom was so excited because this house was cleaner and much larger than the one we had at Mr. Ed's place. This house had four bedrooms, two bedrooms downstairs and two upstairs. The downside was that we had no running water or inside bathroom. Remember this was in the 1950s and I was in the country. We lived outside of the city limits and there was no plumbing in the rural area. Many of the large farms were just beginning to be developed. We had a room to wash-up in, with a large basin, and aluminum bathtub to take a bath. And, for us back then, that was OK.

The morning after the move, we celebrated! Mom and the girls cooked and baked all of Daddy's favorites. We wanted to be sure Daddy knew how happy we all were. Some of Daddy's favorites were Mom's fried chicken, stewed tomatoes, mashed potatoes, and cabbage with country ham.

There were lots of animals on our farm and we had the option of choosing a pet. I chose a chicken named "Pretty". I loved Pretty, but one day there were Pretty's toasted brown legs up in the air on the table. Pretty was all ready for the big feast, but she WAS the feast!!! (LOL). The family laughed about Pretty for a very long time!

Daddy and Mom had seven children and we all had nicknames, that was the country way. There was Junior (Hillary), Lanny (Lankford), Stoop (Stella), Miss Criss (Patricia), Piney (Ronnie), Linda (Linda Lou), and Nancy (Nanny).

When I was growing up, most large farms were owned by white farm owners. The "colored" sharecroppers worked the farm for a small profit, living quarters, food, and credit to support their family's household needs.

Most of the sharecroppers' homes needed work and they did amazing jobs restoring their homes. Water came from a well on the farm and cold spring water from a nearby creek. We didn't think much about the way we lived, there were no families doing much better than us. There were no "poor" people; everyone tried to encourage, protect and inspire each other. They all believed that one day they would own their own farms. God cherished us all.

During the summer, my younger brother, Piney, my younger sister, Nanny, and I would leave the house early in the day, we loved the outdoors. We spent our time playing in the dirt, jumping rope, playing jacks, making mud cakes, climbing trees, and playing hide-and-seek. Occasionally we would ride our neighbor's horses. We wouldn't come home until supper time. That was one meal you didn't want to miss because that food was delicious. We never knew what time it was or what day it was, who cared? We saw the same people in the same place every day! We were fine.

On Sundays, we attended the neighborhood church and we prayed that Daddy would take us to get ice cream after service. On our way to get ice cream, we would sing "This Little Light of Mine".

In September, we prepared to go back to school. The tobacco crop would get sold and Daddy and Mom would take us shopping. The older children always got new clothes and shoes. Black and White bucks (shoes) were my favorite. I don't remember getting very much to go back to school, because the older children came first. Mom made sure the oldest girls got their hair done and the oldest boys got their hair cut. I was included in the younger group of children and Daddy bought us ice cream cones and ginger snap cookies. (LOL).

So, it was back to school in the fall, followed by a fun-filled summer, then back to school again. That was the cycle of life for me – a sharecropper's daughter. And I wouldn't trade it for anything. My memories of those days are filled with joy.

Joy in the Ministry of Healing

By Gail Fields Witherspoon

Joy in the Ministry of Healing

By Gail Fields Witherspoon

As a healthcare worker for over 30 years, I've had countless opportunities to share hope, encouragement, peace and the love of God to patients, co-workers and to complete strangers. In 1 Thessalonians 5:11 it states, "Therefore comfort each other and edify one another, just as you also are doing", NKJV.

I've responded to the voice of God when He has laid on my heart to share with others who needed to hear from Him. I've shared with those who haven't known Him but needed an encouraging word in their moments of darkness. I've even been led to share God's peace in the midst of witnessing death firsthand.

Being obedient to God's voice brings me joy and also brings joy to the people I'm led to minister to. I'd like to share some inspiring moments I've experienced that not only changed the lives of those I've helped, but also changed my life in the process.

I love to minister to children as well as adults. In doing so, I've encountered many children who have been faced with challenges that seem too much for their parents to bare. Yet, in the midst of it all, I have been able to find joy.

I recall a patient I had an opportunity to work with who was diagnosed with autism. She was two years old when I met her and had only a few words in her vocabulary. She demonstrated little to no eye contact, no interaction, and essentially no social skills. Her mother asked if her daughter would ever be able to communicate. I responded by informing her of the medical facts but as I heard her communicate her hopes and dreams, I encouraged her to speak by faith what she wanted for her daughter to be able to accomplish.

Throughout the time I worked with the girl she made phenomenal gains and was eventually able to communicate her needs and wants. She also increased her social skills. She was even able to demonstrate appropriate eye contact and began interacting with others. At the end of her treatment program, her mother expressed her deep gratitude and appreciation for the great things her child had accomplished. She further stated, "You have brought laughter and singing back in our home and my husband and I are much closer". This is a moment that brought tears of joy to my eyes. It was wonderful to know that out of my obedience to the unction of the Holy Spirit, a person's need was answered, and healing was manifested. To this day this little princess is still making phenomenal gains and I continue to marvel at God's handiwork.

In contrast, there are times I've had to minister in tough situations that tugged on the very core of my being. I recall one day while at work I noticed a woman crying. I approached her and asked her what was wrong and she responded by saying that her daughter had just had a baby and she needed help. I asked if she minded if I went to the room to pray for her daughter and she allowed me to do so. To my surprise when I entered the room the baby was stillborn. The mother was overwhelmed with gratitude and thanks, even in the midst of their tremendous loss. Again, I was deeply humbled by the entire experience and, though it was a moment of grief, it was also a moment of joy to be able to be in the right place at the right time to minister comfort and peace in the midst of their storm.

I recall working with a woman in her early forties who had extensive medical complications. As a result, she always appeared to be angry and she often responded negatively to me and others.

One day I attempted to see her and she declined treatment for that day. The very next day when I attempted to work with her, she first apologized for her behavior and began to allow me to work with her. At that time, I suggested that we approach her situation by first finding just one thing that would or could bring her joy in spite of the pain she was experiencing, both emotionally and physically. She agreed and appeared to be pleased about her "new" commitment. Shortly thereafter, I decided to make her an inspirational booklet filled with inspirational messages and affirmations to encourage her. When I presented it to her, her eyes were filled with tears of hope and joy! Her response, "You did this just for me!" expressed her true appreciation, and it was physically witnessed on her countenance.

From that point on she had a new outlook, one of hope and determination. Unfortunately, that time was short-lived because a few weeks later her condition took a turn for the worse. During that time, I was led on my day off to return to work to continue to encourage her. The staff indicated that she had a challenging day and that she was clinging onto life. When I entered her room, she smiled, and I told her how much I loved her and how much of a fighter she was. She didn't say much but I was led to sing to her and continue to provide words of encouragement and peace. The team came in at one point and stated that her vitals had improved and, in their words, "You are an Angel. What a miracle!". The next day she passed away. Though my heart was heavy, I was at peace knowing that I was obedient to the call of the Holy Spirit to render love, compassion, support, comfort and peace to a woman who needed Agape love demonstrated in her life.

Lastly, since COVID-19 has attempted to wage war all other this world, I've had to work with many people who, unfortunately, contracted this virus. One patient I had an opportunity to work with was very upset to learn he was not able to have anything to eat or drink. It was feared that food and liquids could possibly enter his airway, so it was not safe for him to eat or drink anything. This went on for several weeks, and he clearly expressed his frustration.

Despite his negative behavior, I continued to express encouragement and hope to him. He did eventually improve and was able to have a modified diet. It was not very appetizing, but he was able to eat something. To my surprise he was eventually able to begin to express his appreciation and, ultimately, he was able to eat and drink normal consistencies of food and liquids. After he was released to return home, I received an email from him thanking me for "not giving up on him" despite his frustration and the anger he so often displayed. Oh, what joy I felt, it was a moment of gratitude for me and of thankfulness in my heart.

I could go on and on about the countless stories of love and encouragement that I've had the opportunity to experience. Throughout my journey I have provided wholeness, love, comfort, peace, support and victory to those in need. I have also provided, witnessed and received joy through my ministry of healing and, indeed, it has been a joy to do so.

We Wish You Joy

Joy is not a reaction to what happens around you; rather joy is a way of living based upon what happens within you.

As the authors have shared with you...

Joy keeps your faith strong in the face of illness and grief.

Joy encourages you to try new things and grasp fun experiences whenever and wherever they present themselves.

Joy unveils the true meaning behind seemingly ordinary actions and circumstances.

Joy provides peace and direction when life gets difficult.

Joy keeps you going when you would otherwise quit.

I hope that reading the stories in this collection has inspired to you cultivate your own special brand of joy and that you will share it with others. Let's help create a world that allows us to live together peacefully and harmoniously... **In the Key of Joy.**

Project Presenter

Meet the Presenter

GAIL CLANTON

Gail Clanton is president of Clanton Communications, LLC a full-service writing and publishing company located in the Washington, DC area.

She is the author of the Amazon best-seller, *Sparkle In The Rain*, and her writing has appeared in *The Black Woman's Book of Travel and Adventure, Our Fathers Which Art in Heaven*, and *Women Inspiring Nations*.

As a professional writer and editor, Clanton leads writing workshops designed to help people embrace the value of their stories and to more fully recognize the power of their words.

As a speaker, she shares with groups of all sizes from her own experiences, while revealing the strategies she uses to keep her own joy and sparkle intact.

And as a certified professional life coach and a Christian life coach, Clanton helps adults get in touch with their own internal power source so that they gain more complete happiness, success, and joy.

She holds a BA degree in Communication Arts from the University of Dayton, and a MA in Journalism from the Philip Merrill School of Journalism at the University of Maryland, College Park.

Clanton can be reached via her website, Gailclanton.com.

Made in the USA
Middletown, DE
25 June 2021

43122577R00104